How to Detail Diesel Locomotives

Jim Volhard

KALMBACH BOOKS

Printed in the United States of America

97 98 99 00 01 02 03 04 05 06   10 9 8 7 6 5 4 3 2 1

Publisher's Cataloging in Publication
(Provided by Quality Books, Inc.)

Volhard, Jim.
    How to detail diesel locomotives / Jim Volhard. — 1st ed.
    p. cm.
    Includes index.
    ISBN: 0-89024-308-5

    1. Railroads—Models. I. Title.

TF197.V65 1997   625.1'9
                                    QBI97-606

Book design: Mark Watson
Cover design: Kristi Ludwig

▪Contents

▋Introduction

Model railroading is an old and diverse hobby. In the early days there were few, if any, parts available. Early pioneers had to build almost everything from scratch or modify the few parts that were available to customize their models. As model railroading's popularity increased, a few enterprising manufacturers began to produce basic parts. Locomotive, car, and structure building slowly evolved into what became known as a craftsman kit. Wood or metal parts, or a combination of both, were packed with a sheet of instructions showing how to transform the basic materials into a recognizable form.

The hobby maintained its craftsman mindset until the 1950s when the first injection-molded plastic locomotives and cars appeared on the scene. While these early examples were crude by today's standards, they served as a beginning to modern model railroading.

Today, literally thousands of products, parts, and materials are manufactured for the sole purpose of building a model railroad empire. A wide variety of track components, structure kits, and scenery materials are available to build our empires. This part of the hobby continues to be a build-it-yourself proposition. Imagination, ingenuity, and elbow grease combined in equal parts create a stage to run our trains. When it comes to the train itself, our hobby is largely a "ready-to-run" or "shake-the-box" hobby. While there are examples of assembly kits in which the locomotive must be built like a model automobile or aircraft, most locomotives are sold pre-printed and decorated with little if any assembly required.

What was state-of-the-art several years ago has become old news as each new release seems to push the envelope a little further. Even before the locomotive manufacturers took increased realism seriously, some modelers took it upon themselves to improve early plastic locomotives by building detail parts not only to improve the locomotives' appearance but to match details on specific locomotives. By the 1970s, several small manufacturers responded to this

While manufacturers have made great strides in producing accurate, well-detailed models—look at the incredible detail on this out-of-the-box Proto 2000 SW9—most locomotives are not built to these high standards. Modelers must often do extensive work to achieve this level of detail.

movement by producing metal and injection-molded detail parts. Since those early beginnings many more manufacturers have joined those early pioneers, continually adding more new parts.

Open a Walthers catalog to the Super Detailing Parts section or check out the parts rack at a well-stocked hobby shop, and you will encounter a large and varied array of parts. For experienced modelers or those knowledgeable about prototype locomotives, many of the parts are readily identified. Quite a few parts are specific only to locomotives built by a particular manufacturer. Some parts are applied to a large number of locomotive models, while others are limited in application to options specified by a specific prototype railroad. The list of possible applications and reasons for adding parts are nearly endless.

The large number of parts and applications are a boon to the experienced modeler. But where and how does the beginner or inexperienced modeler find the necessary information to accurately add or change details, paint, and weather a model locomotive to match a specific prototype? Detailing a model with extra parts can become expensive and frustrating if you buy the wrong parts or incorrectly locate them. If you are going to go through the effort of modifying or detailing a model, you might as well do it right or at least do it as accurately as the available information allows.

The first step to recreate a miniature version of a full-size locomotive involves research. Without some type of prototype information it is nearly impossible build an accurate model. There are quite a number of sources where you can find information. The best way is to view the actual subject. I recommend that you take photos because you won't be able to recall all the details. Side, end, and overhead shots as well as close-ups of the truck, fuel tank, and other detail-intensive areas will help you later. If you have the equipment, you can videotape the unit. Videos are best as a quick working reference. A high-quality tape can serve as a planning reference for painting and parts location. If you don't have a camera, take notes so you remember specific details, paint condition, and notable weathering effects.

A word of caution. When collecting first-hand data for a project, always respect private property. Whether it be railroad, industrial, or residential property, stay off unless you have permission to be there. Railroad property is a dangerous place and "No Trespassing" signs mean just that. While railroads are becoming more image conscious, they have also become more aggressive in enforcing no trespassing laws to protect their employees, equipment, and the company from litigation-happy clods who injure themselves while trespassing on railroad property. Never enter railroad property without receiving permission in the form of a signed release at a railroad office. Take your photos from public property, streets, grade crossings, and overpasses if possible. Never endanger your safety or anyone else's in the pursuit of information. It is simply not worth it.

Prototype photos and information are available from a variety of sources. Books, magazines, historical society publications, slide and photo dealers, and the Internet can all provide information for a modeling project.

What if the object of your modeling desire is 2,000 miles away and a week-long vacation in pursuit of the beast is out of the question? What if you want to model an older locomotive and the unit, you find, has been repainted, modified, or has long ago been retired and scrapped? There are a number of excellent options available. Books are a good source of information. If you can find one about the specific railroad, there is a good chance it may contain information and photos of the type of engine you're planning to model.

Magazines are an excellent source that cater to both prototype and modeling interests. Prototype-specific magazines are a good source of both the modern and vintage locomotives. Many modeling magazine articles contain both model and prototype photos and information. If current issues don't have what you're looking for, many magazines periodically list available back issues with lists of feature articles.

Another potential source is the local hobby shop. If you are interested in a local railroad, a local hobbyist might have a good collection of photos or slides of the local action and possibly the particular engine you seek. Get to know the proprietor or some of the local modelers. A local club is another place to get information.

If you can't find help locally, attend a large train show, where you might meet photo or slide dealers who may have hundreds or even thousands of slides or photos for sale. Photo and slide dealers also advertise in the classified section of prototype magazines. Find one who specializes in your railroad or region of the country. Catalogs are often available for a nominal fee. Write or call one of these dealers with your specific questions. If they can't help, they may be able to refer you to someone who can.

Parts manufacturers can also be of help. In many cases the parts packages will list prototype applications. Although the instructions may be more general, lacking prototype information, it may be possible to do a credible job of detailing a model using only those instructions.

The newest and possibly the most powerful means of gleaning information is on the Internet with a home computer. As home computers, modems, and on-line access become increasingly user friendly, more and more people are logging on and tapping the virtually limitless information available. While on-line services offer areas for information exchange on a wide variety of subjects including hobbies, the Internet news groups offer the widest scope and variety.

Both prototype and model news groups offer specific areas for discussing both prototype and modeling interests. While these news group areas are not real-time "chat rooms" like those the on-line services provide, you can "post" questions, answers, and comments on the bulletin boards. I have posted a number of question requesting prototype information and have always received answers both in the form of news group postings or through e-mail. In fact, some of the questions have resulted in rather lengthy discussions among those answering, going far beyond the information I originally requested.

In certain news group areas, photos are posted that you can download to your computer and then print. Sending a photo requires special equipment that can scan the photo into the computer memory so it can be posted or e-mailed to someone else. As technology improves, it will become easier and cheaper to take advantage of this incredible source of information.

Once you find prototype information, you can move forward. Now you must determine the goal of the project and what resources you have to accomplish that goal. These two questions become intertwined as subsequent questions and answers help you determine what the finished model will be.

Say, for example, your HO scale layout needs a GP35. What if any models are available? You have several choices. Athearn makes a GP35 and although the unit has a wider-than-scale hood, it is basically a good unit and it sells for about $30. If you don't like the "fat" hood you could replace the Athearn shell with a scale-width hood GP35 shell from Rail Power for about $15. While the Rail Power cab and other details are a little crude compared to today's state-of-the-art models, adding a few basic detail parts will turn this shell into a very nice model. If you decide a major upgrade is in order, you could use the Rail Power shell with Cannon parts and repower with a can motor, but the final price may approach that of the next option. The last option is to purchase a Kato GP35. This is the most detailed, accurate, and best running GP35 available but it has a retail price tag of over $100. If time is more of a constraint than money and you want the most accurate model possible, then the Kato makes the most sense.

A small sample of replacement fans available to the modeler illustrate the fact that accurate prototype information is needed to correctly detail a model.

If you need an SD40-2, however, there is only one option, the Athearn SD40-2. While it is a good model and was state-of-the-art when introduced, it now falls short when compared to today's newest releases. If you want something more than the stock Athearn unit, you will have to modify it. Luckily there are parts available that will bring the Athearn unit up to par with today's best. It just requires money, patience, and elbow grease.

If you need a BN GP39-2, for example, you are out of luck because there are none available. An extensive kitbash is the only way can create an accurate plastic model of this unit.

You will also need to determine how much detail to add. Detailing can be as simple as adding Kadee couplers, a few basic detail parts, and some light weathering to an Athearn factory-painted CSX GP40-2. However if you want to make a more exotic unit, such as a Santa Fe SD26, your ready-to-run options are zero. You will have to commit to a major kitbash. Building an accurately detailed and excellent-running model of such a unit would require parts from a Con-Cor SD24 shell, a Rail Power SD9 shell, the nose and cab from a Proto 2000 GP18, a scratchbuilt hood section with modified

Cannon & Co. doors and hatches, all riding on a A-Line repowered Athearn SD9 frame and trucks and detailed with parts from half a dozen other manufacturers. Obviously, the latter project is considerably more involved than the first, requiring more research, time, skill, and money. Most projects fall somewhere in between these extremes.

As a result, diesel detailing can be classified into four major categories of involvement:

1. Simple detail—adding a few details to a factory-painted unit.
2. Paint and detail—painting and detailing an undecorated unit.
3. Upgrade—replacing cast-on details with more accurate parts, paint, and detail.
4. Kitbash—building an unavailable or poorly modeled unit from a combination of detail parts, parts of other locomotives, and scratchbuilt parts as needed.

Each step up the ladder requires more time, skill, and money, but the end result will be a more accurate model of a particular locomotive.

To accomplish any type of detailing and conversion, you need to know what parts and supplies are available and where to get them. With few exceptions, that source would be the Walthers catalogs. Locomotives, detail parts, and scratchbuilding supplies are all listed in these pages. Photos or illustrations of nearly all parts give the inexperienced modeler a visual clue to identify parts on prototype locomotives. Or better yet, a well-stocked hobby shop may have a selection of the more common detail parts in stock for the modeler to view, making identification of detail parts easier.

Sometimes there are simply no parts available to fill a specific need. Some detective work may then yield a suitable part on some other locomotive. You must determine if the part or complete shell is worth the price. Sometimes you make parts by altering an existing part or by building one from scratch.

The art of building a good-looking and smooth-running locomotive, especially when you go beyond the "off-the-shelf" or "ready-to-run" unit, can involve many diverse operations. This book will help you select and use basic tools, learn new modeling tips and techniques, detail specific areas of a locomotive, and finally paint and finish a locomotive. I hope this book provides you with the basis for many successful modeling projects.

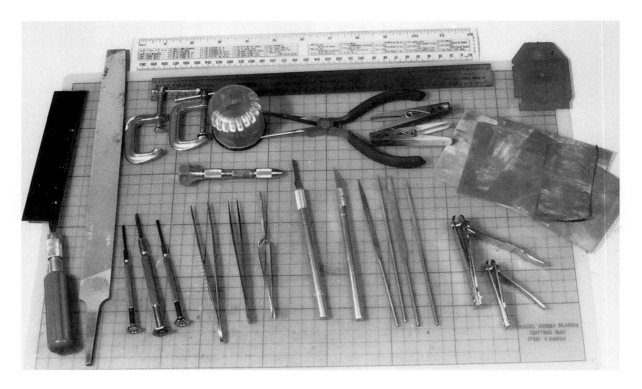

There is no need to go overboard buying tools. A modeler can do professional-quality work with a reasonably priced and carefully chosen set of basic tools.

1 Tools, Techniques, Tips, and Tricks

Tools are the most basic items needed for modeling. Even if you operate nothing but ready-to-run cars and locomotives, you will need a few tools for basic assembly and maintenance. You can spend a fortune on tools, but they are just the means to an end. While it is true up to a point that the more tools you have the easier the job becomes, you don't need a room full of tools to do contest-quality work. With a good basic set of tools, some skill, and patience you can do top-quality work.

The first step is to buy quality tools. A basic set of the right tools is not really that expensive and should be considered an investment rather than an expense. Any extra cost over the "bargain bin" tools will be more than offset by quality and long life. A hobby shop, some large hardware stores, and several specialty tool catalogs will have a good selection of the tools you will need.

WORK AREA

Now that you have collected your modeling tools and materials, you need a place to put them. First you need to determine where you will work. The best place is a permanent workbench where you can put all your tools and supplies in one area so you can spend more time modeling, rather than moving tools and looking for supplies. If you don't have the space, a small desk or table on castors that you can store under a layout or in an unused corner is a good option. If this isn't possible, the last option is to work on an existing table. While it is the least desirable, even this can be an efficient work area if you organize your tools and materials for easy access.

Regardless of where you work, you will need good lighting because it reduces eyestrain, which makes modeling more enjoyable. And most important, we cannot fix what we cannot see. I recommend a low-cost, swing-arm lamp. It provides enough light and its

Tools, fillers, and adhesives

HERE IS A LIST OF THE TOOLS YOU WILL USE MOST FREQUENTLY.

X-acto knives. Buy several no. 1 handles. They are inexpensive and if you have several, you won't need to change blades. The most commonly used blades are the no. 11 and no. 17. Buy a pack of each. While the blades can be re-sharpened, it is best to just throw them out when they are dull.

Tweezers. Buy several different types. Have at least one large one and one small one with a very fine tip.

Files. Get a set of needle files that include several different shapes. Flat, round, semi-round, square, and triangular files all come in handy. An 8" to 10" mill file is great for large surfaces. Be sure to keep the file teeth clean. Soft metal and plastic can clog the teeth. Use a small wire brush to remove clogged material. When files become dull, throw them away and buy new ones.

Miniature screwdrivers. Most sets usually includes a number of different sizes of flat and Phillips screwdrivers.

Clamps. C-clamps, plastic sprung clothespins, and different-sized rubber bands make good clamps.

Pin vise, miniature twist drills, and taps. A pin vise is a small hand-held drill chuck designed to hold tiny drill bits. Miniature drill bits are listed by number rather than size. A chart is useful for choosing a proper bit. You can buy small bits as needed or as a complete set. A popular set contains all bits from no. 80 to no. 61. Taps cut screw threads into metal or plastic. The most commonly used size is a 2-56. You can also buy these individually or in a set.

Side cutters and trimming clippers. Xuron makes a great side cutter that is sold as a track cutter. Its hardened jaws will cut all sorts of wire and thin metal. Toenail and fingernail clippers are great for clipping parts from sprues and trimming away excess plastic.

Razor saws. These are great for sawing bodies apart for kitbashing. You can also cut softer metals with a razor saw. Use a small miter box to make square cuts.

Emery cloth and Flex-i-grit. These are a type of sandpaper with a cloth or plastic backing. Flex-i-grit comes in a pack containing a variety of grit sizes. If you need larger sheets, emery cloth is an alternative. Automotive stores sell the very fine grits you will need. An X-acto sanding stick is handy for sanding in corners and odd places.

NMRA gauge. Using one for the scale you are modeling, you can properly gauge wheels, measure coupler height, and check various track components and clearances.

Measuring tools. A scale ruler, regular 12" ruler, small square, compass, and protractor have many uses. A small micrometer is a useful for thin materials. I use mine more that I ever thought I would.

Vise. While not a must-have item, a small swivel-type vise is very useful for holding large and small parts. Even a small bench vise is handy.

Assorted household tools and utensils. Needle-nose pliers, a small hammer, hack saw, and soldering iron are just a few. Sewing and kitchen tools such as pins, needles, scissors, measuring spoons, and other items are handy at the workbench. Just remember to return your wife's items quickly after using them or, better yet, buy your own.

Power tools. A good first power tool is a variable-speed Moto-tool. This is a useful item for quick removal of metal and plastic. While very effective for removing metal, even the lowest speed creates enough friction to melt the surrounding plastic. If used for only short periods of contact, the Moto-tool removes material without melting plastic. You can add a speed control to further reduce the tool speed to a rate that is safe to use with plastic. A variable-speed drill is also useful, though bulkier than a Moto-tool.

As you assemble your tools, keep in mind that some items can be purchased as need and money dictate. A nice fringe benefit of having these hobby tools is that they come in handy around the house. This is a good bargaining chip when additional tool purchases are questioned by the family accountant.

In addition to tools for removal and destruction, you will need a number of items to put everything back together. There are many products that I have not used that may be as good or even better that those I am using. So don't be afraid to try something new.

Liquid cement. Use this for plastic-to-plastic joints. I use Testor's brand for most applications. Its slower setting time lets you make adjustments before it sets. I use Tenax 7R when I need it to set quickly. Its quick-setting quality makes it more difficult to work with. Tenax is very thin and evaporates quickly. Because it is so thin, capillary action is rapid. If you use your fingers to hold the part, be careful that the glue doesn't get under your fingers and ruin the finish.

While styrene is the most commonly used plastic, there are other types of plastics. ABS, butyrate, and acrylic are a few you can use for modeling. But some liquid cements will not bond some of these materials. If you have a bonding problem, check the manufacturer's recommendation.

Cyanoacrylates (super glue) or CA. The most common use is for metal-to-plastic joints. My favorite brand is Goldberg Slow Jet. This thick CA is easy to apply and is excellent for filling gaps. In fact, I use it as a filler in some applications. If I need to speed the setting time, I use Goldberg's Jet Set or Pacer Technologies Zip Kicker. I use a toothpick or small brush to apply them because they can damage plastic surfaces if sprayed on. Jet DeSolv works well for debonding mistakes, including those involving fingers. I rarely use Super Jet or any other thin super glue because they are difficult to work with.

5-Minute epoxy. Epoxy is an adhesive with two parts that must be mixed in equal portions to initiate the bonding process. Use it for metal-to-metal or metal-to-plastic joints where strength is important.

Silicone sealer. While not a primary adhesive, it does have its applications. It is most useful in remotoring projects to attach the motor to the frame. When fully cured, it allows the motor some movement and absorbs vibration that would otherwise be transferred to the chassis.

Fillers. Squadron Green Putty is a widely available product to fill gaps, low spots, or damaged areas. However, many fillers shrink. Unless you use thin coats and let them dry thoroughly for several days, finished areas will continue to shrink and develop lows spots. Worse yet, you might finish and paint before you detect the shrinkage. I have been guilty of such haste and have "sink-holes" in several models to prove it. Most fillers are softer than the styrene plastic they are applied to, so be careful when sanding a filled area that you don't remove too much filler. I haven't tried auto body fillers, but several modeling articles have mentioned specific brands and the authors have had excellent results. As I mentioned before, I use thickened CA as a filler also. This material does a great job on many applications, especially metal. Its best assets are speed and that it does not shrink after it has set hard. Apply CA and let it set for an hour or until it isn't tacky before filing and sanding. If you let the CA cure completely it becomes very hard and is more difficult to finish.

Miscellaneous materials. Walthers Goo is a useful material, as it bonds nearly anything to anything. White and yellow Elmer's glues are great for wood and paper.

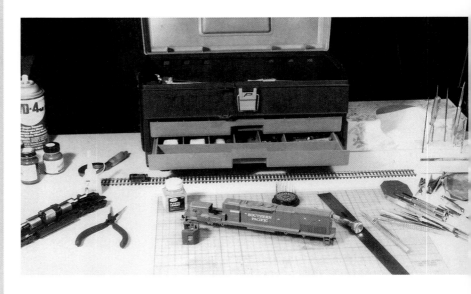

1-1. A tidy modeling area with properly stored tools is conducive to good modeling.

adjustability lets you put the light where you need it.

While it is not necessary, another useful item is a low-power optical visor. I have an inexpensive pair and wouldn't model without them. The magnification has eased strain on my eyes considerably. It also helps me see flaws that would sometimes escape detection until the model was painted.

Organizing your work area is the key to efficient work, whether you have a permanent or nomadic site. All the space in the world is useless unless you maintain some degree of order. A tool box, tool caddie, or even a fishing tackle box is useful for storing tools. Access to tools is important. You should also store supplies such as paints, brushes, glues, and other frequently used items where they can be easily accessed. Leave styrene, wood strips, and shapes in their plastic packaging and store them in a small box or on end in one of those inexpensive magazine-organizing bins found in department stores. You can store quite a few bags in one of these and it keeps them somewhat organized. Those small organizer cabinets with clear drawers are great for storing detail parts, screws, and other small items that seem to multiply as the railroad grows. Leave extra parts in their bags so

you can identify them later. Just be sure to sort the parts in some type of order and label the drawers. It does no good to have a supply of parts on hand if you can't find anything.

A frequently mentioned, but seldom discussed, modeling item is the scrapbox. This need be nothing more than a cardboard box where you place unused and unneeded parts, pieces, shells, and cut apart remains of kit-bashing projects for possible future use. While you probably won't use most of them, there will be times when you will find a part that is perfect for a particular application. While it doesn't need a prominent location, it should be readily accessible for continued donations and search-and-rescue missions.

SAFETY

For all the satisfaction and pleasure our hobby can provide, careless use of modeling products can cause accidents, injuries, or long-term health problems. Safety is nothing more than common sense. While you probably don't need a list of dos and don'ts posted on your work area wall, **you should religiously follow manufacturers' warnings and recommendations.** Modeling workbenches are literally a household hazard. With paints, thinners, solvents adhesives, and sharp tools abounding, there are countless accidents waiting to happen.

Your number one concern should be for the safety of others in the household. The vapors from carelessly used petroleum-based products and solvents can put everyone in the home at risk. If small children are in the house or visit frequently, all chemical-based products, sharp tools, and small parts should be put away between work sessions or at least be placed out of reach. One moment of carelessness can lead to a lifetime of regret.

Your safety is also at risk. Solvents and petroleum-based paints have harmful vapors that can be toxic in high concentrations. While there may not be any immediate effects, many toxins can accumulate in the body and can have serious future consequences. Make sure you have adequate ventilation and wear a mask or respirator when working with these products. Do aerosol and airbrush painting only in a ventilated paint booth. Petroleum products and solvents are also fire hazards. Poor ventilation can lead to high concentrations of vapors which can become explosive. Knives and X-acto blades pose a danger. While rarely life-threatening, a nasty finger cut can ruin an evening. Wear safety glasses when using power tools and even some hand tools.

Many accidents, including those during modeling, are the result of carelessness and haste. When you don't take time for safety, chances are you will spend that time later looking for a bandage, cleaning up a mess, or fixing something that broke. The quality of your modeling will also suffer from haste. You've heard the old railroad slogan "safety is no accident." Keep that and common sense in mind and your modeling sessions will be safe, enjoyable, and productive.

TECHNIQUES

In the course of your modeling projects you will work with many materials. Several types of plastics, metals, wood, cardstock, and paper may cross your workbench during the course of a project. Your ability to work

1-2. Organize and store parts and supplies so they are easily accessible, and you can spend more time modeling rather than looking for things.

with these materials will determine the success or failure of each project.

Working with styrene. By far the most commonly used medium for the average modeler is styrene plastic. Styrene can be sawed, cut, carved, drilled, tapped, sanded, polished, and painted. While it doesn't have the strength of metal, it is much easier to work with. It has dimensional stability, is not affected by moisture, and when used

for injection molding, it reproduces the finest details. Styrene's major weakness is its inability to withstand heat. Working with hand tools seldom causes problems but high-speed power tools will cause difficulty. The following is a list of basic styrene working skills and a description of each.

Cutting. When you're working with sheet styrene up to .040" thick, the most effective means of cutting is the

1-3. An unorganized and messy work area is neither efficient nor safe to work in.

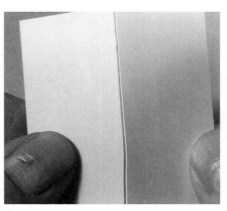

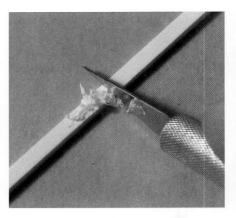

1-4. An effective way to cut sheet styrene is with the score-and-snap method. Use a no. 11 X-acto blade to score the cut line. Cut it with several light passes.

1-5. The cut line is now snapped and the styrene will be broken cleanly through. Clean up any remaining rough edges with a file or sandpaper.

1-6. To remove thin layers of plastic, scrape with a knife blade while holding it at a 90-degree angle.

score-and-snap method. To use this method, mark the sheet and use a metal straightedge to make a number of light cuts with a no. 11 X-acto blade, each a little deeper than the previous one. Then hold the sheet and snap the scored line through. The result should be a clean, straight edge. Smooth rough spots with a file or sandpaper. Make irregular or special shapes using this method. When the score-and-snap method will not work, mark your work and cut as before, but cut progressively deeper until the sheet severs. Patience is required, especially on thicker sheets.

Small-dimensional styrene strips are also best cut with a sharp knife. Another method useful for such things as window openings is to mark the opening and drill holes around the inside of the marking. Then punch out the scrap material and finish the opening to the marks with files. On thinner sheet material cut the styrene with a sharp scissors.

Sawing. This is the most useful method for cutting apart body shells for kitbashing. Both razor saws and jeweler's saws work well. A razor saw will cut straighter because of its thin, wide blade, but a jeweler's saw will cut deeper because of its deep throat. To cut apart a body shell, mark the cut and start cutting with the razor saw. Start with short strokes until the cut has

been established, then lengthen it. Take your time and check your progress to make sure the cut is straight. If possible, cut a small distance from the mark. When finished, use a file to remove the rest of the material up to the mark.

Sawing is also the preferred method for cutting heavier styrene dimensional strips and structural shapes. Use a razor saw and a small miter box to ensure straight, square cuts.

Filing. After cutting and sawing, filing is the next most efficient method of removing material. When filing a flat surface, use the largest file you can. This serves two purposes. It's an efficient way to remove material, and it will more likely result in a true and flat surface. Filing large items works best if you can clamp the part in a vise so you can use two hands to file and apply even pressure to the surface. On small parts one hand is usually sufficient to control the file. Whether you're using one hand or two, try to keep even pressure on your work and check your progress often.

Files are cutting tools, and like all cutting tools they become dull with use. When this happens throw them out. A dull file is inefficient and frustrating to use. But do not confuse a dull file with one that is clogged with material. Remove the offending material with a small wire brush.

Scraping. Scraping is similar to filing, but you remove material with a nearly perpendicular knife blade. This is a useful method when there is little or no room to use a file. Scraping is also a good method to remove details from a body shell. Hold the knife blade at about a 90-degree angle to the surface and start scraping away the material. Different styles of X-acto blades may come in handy for different scraping applications. Stop scraping when the material is nearly removed and finish the job with sandpaper.

Sanding. This is probably the most underemphasized of the basic skills. Regardless of what you cut, file, fill, and scrape, if the final sanding is not done properly or completely, you will be disappointed with the results. Sanding is the finishing process that reduces the imperfections on our models to a point where they become inconsequential or invisible. My favorite sanding medium is Flex-i-grit, made by K&S Engineering. I hesitate to call it sandpaper because it has a flexible plastic backing instead of paper. Emery cloth is also useful but its thin cloth backing isn't as easy to control as Flex-i-grit. An "A" pack of Flex-i-grit contains five sheets of assorted grades from coarse to super-fine for finishing. Another handy sanding item is the X-Acto Sanding Stick. These narrow belts of sandpaper

Cast-on grills have been removed by scraping and sanding

1-7. A full complement of grills are cast on the Rail Power C30-7 body shell. To match certain prototype locomotives, some of these grills must be removed. This can be done effectively by first slicing off as much grill as possible with a no. 17 X-acto blade. Then scrape the area smooth with the same blade. Finish with wet-sanding. When carefully done, this method leaves no marks.

1-8. Add a small amount of water when using sandpaper to keep the removed material from clogging the grit. This method is called wet-sanding.

that mount on a plastic stick are handy for sanding in confined areas. You can accomplish the same thing by wrapping sandpaper around a stick, but the tool's ease of use more than justifies owning one.

To sand styrene or any plastic material you must wet-sand. Apply a small amount of water to the sandpaper or part before sanding. The water keeps the sanded-off plastic material from clogging the grit and serves as a lubricant. Sanding without water is inefficient because you will have to continually remove the clogged grit from the sandpaper.

Choosing the correct grit for the job will depend on the condition of the surface to be sanded. A rough and irregular surface will require a coarse grit to quickly remove material. When you attain the proper shape, switch to the next finer grade and continue sanding. Do not switch to the next finer grade until the scratches from the previous paper are removed. Continue this process down to the finest sheet. If done properly, you will have a super finish that blends in perfectly with the surrounding area. If you create low spots, cracks, or other blemishes, rework the area by filling, filing, and sanding. Remember, this is the final

finished surface. Paint will not mask flaws visible to the naked eye.

Drilling. There aren't too many rules or tricks to drilling. It is best to use sharp bits and keep the speed low. Throw dull bits away. They are not that expensive. Small bits are quite fragile, so use light pressure and keep the bit properly aligned. Excess side pressure is often fatal to small bits. Keeping the speed low is not a problem if you use a hand-held pin vise, but excess speed with a power drill will soften and melt the plastic around the hole. Use only a variable speed tool at low rpm.

Tapping. This is the process of cutting threads for a screw into a previously drilled hole. This is a straightforward operation. Use a chart that shows the proper size hole to be drilled to choose the tap. Chuck the tap in the pin vise and begin to turn the tap into the hole, making sure the tap is aligned with the hole. After several turns back the tap out and clean the debris off the tap. Repeat this operation until you are down to the complete threads on the tap. Plastic is much softer than metal, so be careful not to strip the threads when cutting them. The hole is now ready to accept the screw.

Stretching sprue. Sprue is the leftover plastic runners from a plastic model kit, which can be used a number of ways when stretched. Heat a length of sprue over a small flame, pull or stretch

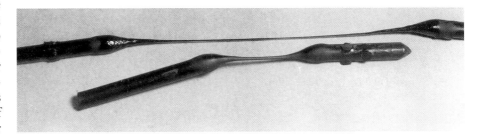

1-9. You can easily stretch sprue by heating it. It will stretch differently depending on how hot it gets. The top sprue was heated quite a bit, so when it was stretched it formed a long, thin string with little taper except at the ends. The lower sprue was heated much less, so when stretched it produced a sharply tapered piece.

the softened plastic into thin threads of plastic, and let it cool. With a little practice you can produce everything from heavy tapers to almost hairlike threads. I find stretched sprue most useful for plugging holes. When the sprue has a slight taper, it can be pushed snugly into the hole and secured with liquid cement. When the cement has set, trim the protruding end flush, file, and wet-sand the area to a smooth finish.

Working with metal. There are several types of metals that are commonly used on model railroads. Die-cast metal is mostly used for locomotive frames. It is quite hard, though not as hard as steel. It's fairly easy to saw, file, and drill. White or lead-based metal is often used for casting detail parts when strength is not a primary concern. It is very soft and easy to work. Be careful not to break the parts when working with them.

Brass is a common modeling metal. It is used for casting detail parts when strength is a major concern. Brass sheets, strips, and structural shapes are readily available. Brass is a useful metal because it's easy to work with and easy to solder. Steel and aluminum are seldom used for modeling purposes.

Cutting and sawing. Cutting and sawing metal is not difficult. Use a hacksaw for heavier materials and a razor saw for lighter materials and brass structural shapes. Cut thin sheet brass with sharp shears or scissors.

Filing. The same basic rules for filing plastic apply to metal. Soft metals such as white metal castings and some die-cast locomotive frames will quickly clog file teeth. A wire brush may not remove all the pieces. Use a tip of a knife to pick out debris.

Sanding. Sanding metal is very similar to sanding plastic. Use water or a light oil to wet-sand surfaces.

Drilling. Drilling metal is also very similar to drilling plastic. Use more pressure and sharp bits. Drilling very small holes is difficult. Even, steady pressure is a must. Even a slight tug can snap a small bit.

Tapping. Again, similar to plastic, except you must apply more pressure to cut the threads.

Soldering. This is a simple operation in which you can join certain non-ferrous metals using a soft metal called solder that has been heated to a molten state. This molten metal flows between the mating surfaces and, when cool, forms a strong joint. For modeling purposes, metals including brass, copper, and nickel-silver are all easily soldered.

Soldering is easy. Clean the parts to be joined of dirt and tarnish. Apply a small amount of petroleum-jelly-like material called soldering flux to the intended joints. Use a soldering iron or a small torch to heat the parts. Touch the solder, which comes in wire form, to the parts to be joined. When the parts are hot enough, the solder will melt and flow into the joint. Remove the heat. When the joint cools sufficiently the solder will solidify to complete the joint.

Soldering has many applications in model railroading. The most common use is for wiring our railroads. Solder provides a hard, solid, highly conductive joint between track components, wire, and the power source. You must use a rosin-core type solder for all electrical connections. Soldering is used almost exclusively to construct imported brass engines. For model detailing purposes it has limited use unless the modeler is building up brass parts. It is used more for wiring in model locomotives.

That pretty much sums up the basic tools and techniques needed for modeling. If any of these are new to you, practice on something old or broken to master—or at least become acquainted with—the tools and methods described. As you gain experience your confidence and skill will improve accordingly. You will develop your own favorite methods and techniques to solve modeling problems. The most important tip to remember is to be patient. Live by this rule and success is almost guaranteed.

TIPS & TRICKS

The art of modeling is a combination of many things. You need knowledge of the prototype to build accurate models. You must also develop skills to work with building mediums (plastic, metal, wood, etc.), as well as patience, persistence, and the ability to think through problems.

Developing and improving modeling skills is usually a direct function of experience. The more you build, the more proficient you will become. This is true with any activity you undertake. Once a task becomes second nature you will be able to perform operations with little thought, making the procedure quick and easy. What has all this got to do with model railroading? An inexperienced modeler may decide that the short hood needs to be replaced on a locomotive. With a razor saw in hand, the modeler looks at the situation. That step in the nose poses some potential problems. How does he cut that step or jog in the nose so as not to damage the surrounding area and details?

By the time the novice modeler begins the first saw cut, an experienced modeler would likely have the nose removed and the walkway area cleaned up and be ready to install the new nose. In similar fashion, two modelers intend to replace the cast-on grab irons with

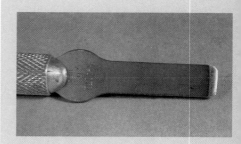

1-10. Removing the corners on a no. 17 X-acto blade will lessen the chances of damaging the surrounding surface when removing smaller details from flat surfaces. This modified blade works well for removing cast-on grab irons.

1-11. To kitbash an ATSF SD26 you will need several higher hood doors. Use two Cannon & Co. doors (on the right) to make a higher door. Cut the doors apart and reassemble them into the high door configuration. Careful cutting and sanding will make the splice nearly invisible.

1-12. Salvage detail parts from old shells. Use a razor or saw to cut the parts from the shell.

more accurate wire parts. The experienced modeler grabs the X-acto knife with a modified no. 17 blade and routinely slices off the grabs while leaving the accurate mounting-nut part of the casting neatly on the shell rather than replacing it also. The inexperienced modeler finally decides on an unmodified no. 17 blade, but this has sharp corners. While he's slicing the grabs from the body, his blade's sharp corners gouge and nick the body in numerous places. A number of the mounting-nut castings get sliced off. All these mistakes take time and effort to repair, not to mention frustrating the modeler.

Patience and persistence in modeling is also important. Mistakes and errors in judgment are inevitable. Sometimes you will be well into a project before you encounter an unforeseeable complication, rendering a great deal of work unusable. It takes a great deal of patience to keep a project from bouncing off the wall at a time like that. Many times even the most experienced modelers come upon situations that seem difficult to overcome. Sometimes a problem is so confounding that you'll

need to set the project aside because you can't come up with a solution. I have had quite a number of these episodes. While such a project is on the back burner, you will think about the problem from time to time. One day you might come up with the answer and resume the project. Then there are problems that don't get resolved. If you are lucky, some manufacturer may solve the problem for you by producing a part or an entire locomotive. If not, it may stay on the back burner permanently. I have several such projects and my only hope is that some manufacturer will solve my problem.

Altering existing parts and details. The main theme of this book, diesel detailing, might imply that every cast-on or stock part that has a more accurate or detailed after-market counterpart should be replaced. This is not true. While many applications may dictate taking this route, each potentially replaceable part should be studied. Is anything wrong with the existing part? Is it a major detriment to the model? Is it barely noticeable or nearly invisible to the naked eye—but knowing it's there bothers you? Could you the modify the part so it's accurate or at least acceptable? Consider the following scenario.

While a number of detail manufacturers produce replacement locomotive cabs in nearly perfect scale

dimension of the real thing, take a moment to consider what you really want to change before tossing the original into the trash. If you simply want the most accurate cab possible, the original cab should be scrapped. If it bothers you that the windows on the original cab sit too deeply into the frame due to the thickness of the cab walls, then there are ways to save time and money while fixing them.

Several companies make replacement "glass" that fits the openings and brings the windows flush with the cab exterior as on the prototype. If the new windows are adequate, you have saved a few dollars that can be used elsewhere, plus the time needed to build the replacement cab.

Altering detail parts. Many times in the course of detailing, situations arise where no accurate part is available to fit a certain application. Before resigning yourself to scratchbuilding it, look at available detail parts to see if any can be modified or altered to do the job. If planned well and carefully done the altered parts need not be of lower quality than the original. With enough care the modification won't be visible.

While building a model of a Santa Fe SD26 I ran across such a situation. When the ATSF railroad rebuilt their aging SD24s, they made quite a few modifications. The prototype hood

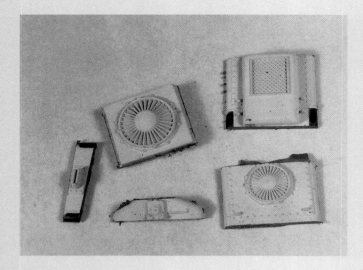

1-13. Finish trimming the removed parts. A toenail clipper will work well to trim material right up to the edge of the part.

1-14. Use a large file or coarse sandpaper to remove the remaining material from the back of the part. These parts are now ready for installation.

section had several access doors and internal filter screens on its sides and an internal filter hatch and exhaust stack on the roof. In studying this new area, I determined that I could use replacement filter screens and a GP35 door and plate as is. The internal filter hatch and access doors were another matter.

The new parts are not 100 percent accurate but it would not have been possible to scratchbuild doors with anything close to the level of detail that exist on the replacement parts.

If you can modify existing parts you can usually save quite a bit of time compared to scratchbuilding parts. As an added bonus, if properly done, the parts can be as high-quality as the original part. This greatly expands the potential of an already large supply of detail parts.

Salvaging parts. There are several reasons to salvage parts from another engine. The parts to be removed may be unique with no commercial equivalent, or you may wish to save money. A salvaged engine may contain many parts for a detailing project, and the cost of that engine or shell may be considerably lower than buying all the detail parts separately. You may also have an engine that has been damaged or is not being used or needed. Rather than letting this investment sit unused,

use it. The drive train can be used for other repair jobs and the shell may have usable parts. In fact, real railroads reuse scrapped parts. Older models of sidelined locomotives are cannibalized to keep the rest of the fleet running. Even newer locomotives, if they are wrecked and written off, are stripped of usable parts.

Scrapping a locomotive is not difficult at all. Remove the chassis or drive train. Complete trucks, sideframes, gears, wheels, drive shafts, flywheels, and the motor are all potentially usable parts. Even save the chassis.

Removing plastic parts from shells and preparing them for reuse is not difficult at all. All you need is some elbow grease and a little care. Cut the parts you need from the shell using a razor saw. The photos show the sequence of saw cuts to remove parts from an Athearn HO scale GP7 body. The "fat hood" Geep is of little use to the serious modeler, but the parts that can be salvaged from such a shell are quite good.

After the parts are separated from the shell, prepare them for reuse. This involves removing body parts that are not needed. Trim away as much material as possible before grinding, filing, or sanding off the rest. Use a coarse file to remove the bulk of the material. When

you are almost finished, switch to a less coarse file or use sandpaper secured to a flat surface to remove the remaining material. When all the material has been removed, you can install the part.

If you are just scrapping a shell and have no immediate use for the removed parts, save them, but don't bother removing the excess material until you have a use for the parts.

In many cases it would be better to leave the shell intact and only remove needed parts. That way you are not limiting your options for the remaining shell. Some day you might need a part of a hood, group of doors, boarding steps, or the entire walkway frame area. Saving the shell in the scrap box keeps those options alive.

Scratchbuilding parts. There are times when there are no available aftermarket parts, scrap parts from another shell, or parts that can be modified to match a specific prototype part. Your choices are to ignore it, use the closest available part, or build one. While the thought of building a part or assembly can be daunting to the beginner, it is really not that difficult. Start with something simple and as you gain experience move on to more involved projects.

There are a number of benefits to building your own parts. First, you can build something different. Not being constrained by what's on the hobby shop shelf, you can tackle a unique kit-bash—something that none of the boys down at the club layout have. Second, scratchbuilding improves modeling skills. While detailing our locomotives is a step above using only ready-to-run equipment on our railroads, there is no exceptional skill involved in clipping a commercial part from a sprue and cementing it in place. The ability to build your own gives you freedom from the packaged parts. No longer will you look at a potential modeling project and find reasons why it cannot be done; if you can build what cannot be bought, you will see the reasons why it *can*. A third reason is cost. The cost of raw materials used for scratchbuilding are usually minimal. Building your own parts is probably the greatest bargain in the entire hobby.

Making your own parts to save money. While model railroading is an extremely enjoyable hobby, it can get very expensive. High-priced items like $100 locomotives, $15 cars, $20 turnouts, and $40 building kits do serve to highlight the financial side of the hobby. Most modelers have some type of budget or at least a general amount they can spend. If you are only building locomotives as a hobby obviously all dollars flow into this area. If you are building a layout, many different areas are competing for a finite amount of money. One way to stretch dollars is to economize. While the common perception of economizing usually means cheaper or lower quality, that does not have to be the case with diesel detailing. There are a number of parts you can make that will compare favorably with commercial parts. The primary consideration here is time. If time is in short supply, then making parts that can be bought is not efficient. If time is of little consequence, then some savings can be realized by making certain parts. In fact, making parts may result in a more accurate model. Instead of using the commercial parts that are "close enough," you can make them as accurate as possible.

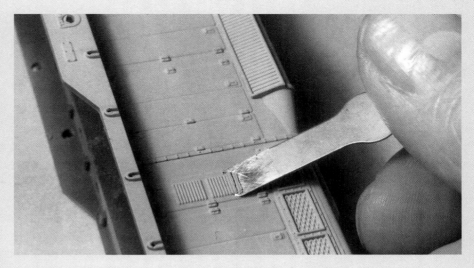

1-15. Remove some thin details by shaving them off with a no. 17 X-acto blade. If it's carefully done the parts can be reused. This is a useful skill—sometimes parts such as latches, hinges, and louvers must be moved. Reattach the shaved-off parts with liquid cement.

Some parts that are easy to make include grab irons and coupler cut levers. The standard drop grab irons generally run about 10 cents apiece. Using brass wire they can be made for a couple of cents each. If you plan on making quite a few of them, make a simple bending jig to speed the process and give the parts uniformity. Commercial coupler cut levers run around a quarter apiece. Using the same wire you can bend your own for less than a nickel.

These are just a few examples of scratchbuilding parts. Whether you are building parts because no commercial part is available, to economize, or just because you like to build things, scratchbuilding is interesting and a key part to the art of diesel detailing.

While on the subject of economy, there are a number of things a modeler can do to keep costs down. One method is careful shopping. If you are fortunate enough to live in an area with several hobby shops you may find price differences on some items. Train shows are another good place to find savings. Vendors often have a good selection and prices are quite reasonable because the competition is right across the aisle. Mail order is another possibility. Prices can be very reasonable but problems with back-orders, credit, and shipping

can cause headaches far beyond any savings realized.

One consideration when buying from out-of-town vendors and mail-order houses is concern about defective products and warranties. While most if not all manufacturers' products are warranted against defective materials and workmanship, the hassle of returning the defective items to the seller can be significant. If you bought your locomotive at the local hobby shop the proprietor may fix the problem right there or swap the defective item for one that works. Sometimes saving money does carry a price tag that is not visible at the time of purchase.

A swap meet can also be a source of savings if there is one in your area. Most participants bring items they no longer use or need. Some may even be getting out of the hobby and are disposing of all their supplies. Some very good used items can be found that with a little cleaning will look and operate like new. A gold mine of parts may be found in junk boxes. Here, either at a price per part deal or one price takes all, there can be many useful items. While you might not need many items immediately, you can organize and store them for future use in your scrapbox.

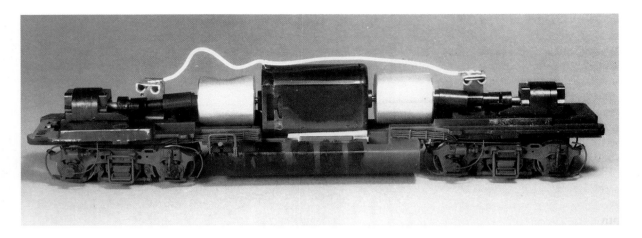

This Athearn GP40-2 underframe has been upgraded with an A-Line repower kit. Adding a can motor and using the tune-up procedures in this chapter will make your Athearn locomotive run as well as any locomotive made.

2 Basic Tune-Up

While this book deals primarily with the appearance of scale models, their operation is also of great importance. Because you want an engine that runs as well as it looks, you must understand how an engine runs and be able to maintain, repair, or improve it.

Fortunately, many new engines are great runners right out of the box. Place any new Kato engine on the track and slowly open the throttle. The engine will respond from a barely perceptible crawl to a reasonably close-to-scale top speed in a smooth, quiet manner. Motor and gear noise are nearly absent. The only harsh sounds will be the clicking of the steel wheels over rail joints. Some train set companies have responded to the demand for improved performance and appearance by offering an upgraded line of locomotives. Bachmann's SPEC-TRUM line and Life-Like's PROTO 2000 series are two notable examples. In general, you get what you pay for. When I pay $100 dollars for a plastic diesel

locomotive I expect it to run like a Swiss watch. When I pay $35 for an Athearn engine, while it runs very well, I don't expect the same results.

There are engines sold in the Athearn price range, but they are definitely "train set" locomotives. They may have decent shells, which may be of some use to the modeler, but their drive trains are inferior to those of the better-quality locomotives. Avoid locomotives that have the motor built right into one of the trucks (photo 2-1) or have no separate frame. Some locomotives have the standard motor, drive shaft, and truck arrangement, but the components are of poor quality and will not run reliably very long. Another option to avoid is the traction tires that claim to increase pulling power. These soft tires don't stay perfectly round, so the locomotive will wobble down the tracks—and they do not pick up power, making continuous electrical contact more difficult. To avoid buying one of the inferior locomotives,

especially if you're a beginner, seek the help of a knowledgeable modeler or buy your locomotives from a reputable hobby shop.

All quality locomotive drives operate the same way. A motor produces the power, which is transferred by way of a drive shaft at each end to the locomotive truck. A universal joint on each drive shaft lets the trucks turn and swivel. Once the power reaches the trucks a worm-and-spur-gear combination reduces the motor speed and transfers the power to the wheels. Electrical power is picked up through the wheels and is routed to the motor terminals. Though the way this is accomplished varies from company to company, the left and right side wheels of the locomotive must be electrically insulated from each other.

One performance-enhancing feature on all quality locomotives is the flywheel, usually made from brass or some similar metal. The flywheels are attached to the motor shafts. Any changes in motor speed are buffered by the mass of the spinning flywheel. Without flywheels any change in throttle setting results in an almost immediate and unprototypical change in speed. The spinning flywheels keep the locomotive running smoothly at constant speed, and even with momentary breaks in electrical contact caused by dirty wheels or track irregularities. The flywheels are intended to be performance enhancers. They are not intended to cover up for poor or erratic locomotive performance.

When you purchase a new locomotive, unless you need to complete some critical assembly, you will probably put it on the rails about as fast as the box can fall back to the table. The throttle opens and your new power begins to traverse the layout. Only then do the instructions get opened. While manufacturers have made great strides in locomotive performance, the quality of the instructions that come with them has lagged behind. Only the more recent Life-Like PROTO 2000 locomotives have a comprehensive set of instructions explaining break-in, lubrication, cleaning, and periodic maintenance, in addition to an exploded view of the locomotive and parts list. Most manufacturers' instructions only contain an exploded view of the locomotive, a parts list, and simple assembly instructions. Although the absence of adequate instructions is not really all that critical, it is nice to have something to refer to when it comes time for disassembly or regular, preventive maintenance.

WHEEL GAUGE

The first item that should be checked on any locomotive is the wheel gauge. Use the NMRA gauge and check each axle for proper gauge (photo 2-2). This is vitally important, as anything but exact gauge will cause problems. For the most part new locomotives' wheels are in gauge. Should any axles need attention, remove the cover from the bottom of the truck to reach the offending wheel set. On some units (Kato and Atlas), the gearbox cover can be removed only by first removing the

2-1. This shell includes an inferior drive, which should be replaced with a higher-quality drive.

body and reaching down through between the frame and the top of the truck and lifting the retaining tabs with a small screwdriver. Remove the truck sideframes and pull off the wheel wipers from the ends of the axles to free the wheels. Gently push or pull the wheel while turning it. Do this until the wheel flanges fit exactly into the grooves of the gauge. Be sure the center plastic drive gear remains centered with regard to the wheels or problems may occur when you reassemble the truck.

COUPLER ADJUSTMENT

The other main concern is coupler and uncoupler pin height. Whether you use the kit-supplied couplers or install Kadee couplers, the height of the trip or uncoupling pin is important. If the pin is too low and it hangs between the rails, it will snag trackwork and uncoupling ramps and cause derailments. In the case of Kadee couplers, the trip pin is easily adjusted with a needle-nose pliers or a Kadee trip pin adjustment pliers.

The height of the coupler knuckle is important for mating with other couplers. Dissimilar coupler heights will cause unscheduled uncouplings. A Kadee coupler height gauge (photo 2-3) is indispensable for properly adjusting the Kadee style couplers. You can adjust the knuckle height by shimming or removing material from the coupler mounting pad.

2-2. Accurately gauged wheels will fit perfectly into the flange grooves on an NMRA gauge. Anything less than perfect should be adjusted—there is simply no room for compromise.

The coupler should move easily in its mounting and center itself. If not, a touch of powdered graphite may do the trick. If this doesn't work, disassemble the coupler. The centering spring may be damaged or the coupler box may be too tight to let the coupler move easily. This is especially important when you use the delayed uncoupling feature. All components must work properly for smooth, trouble-free operation.

BREAK-IN

To break in your locomotive, run your locomotive at varying speeds in both directions for at least an hour. If your layout is designed for continuous running, let your locomotive run laps at

2-3. Use a Kadee coupler height gauge to measure both the height of the coupler knuckle and the trip pin. The coupler knuckle should mate perfectly with the coupler on the Kadee gauge. The trip pin must not extend below the plate on the bottom of the gauge or the pin will snag track work. If the pin is bent up too high, it may not uncouple properly over a Kadee uncoupling magnet.

2-4. Check gears for flash and damaged or malformed teeth. Small bits of flash at the edge of the mounting hole may interfere with gear movement. Trim this with a sharp no. 11 X-acto blade.

varying speeds and directions. The break-in will serve to seat the motor brushes, evenly distribute lubricant, and take a little edge off the new gears that may show itself as "tightness" when the unit runs. In fact, locomotive performance should continue to improve slightly after parts wear into place.

If you really want your locomotive broken in thoroughly, there are several other steps that involve tearing down the entire drive train. There are several reasons to do this. The first is that most manufacturers are a little overzealous when it comes to lubrication. Some new locomotives are literally dripping with oil. All this excess lubricant is almost magnetic when it comes to dirt. Remove this mess and apply a suitable lubricant in the proper places and in proper amounts. The other reason is that disassembly lets you inspect all the drive train parts for flaws and proper fit.

DISASSEMBLY AND TUNE-UP

To disassemble a model, follow the manufacturer's directions when possible. In the absence of instructions, study the exploded view of the model to discover clues to any hidden screws, clips, or tabs that hold the parts together. The first step is to remove the body from the chassis. On some locomotives you may need to remove the couplers before doing this. Once the shell is free, check for any wiring between it and the chassis. Remove any printed circuit boards, electronics, or lights if possible. These items are normally mounted with screws. There should be some sort of clip or provision for removing the wire from the motor. Remove the trucks next. There is usually some sort of worm gear retainer clip that holds both the truck and worm gear in place. You will probably need a small flat-bladed screwdriver to pry the cover loose. Be careful not to lose the worm gear bearings, spacing washers, or drive shaft parts. The truck should now drop from the chassis.

The drive shaft components can now be examined for problems. You'll find that drive shafts vary from manufacturer to manufacturer. On Athearn and similar models check that the drive shaft halves freely telescope into each other. Also check that the universal joints are not so tight that they can't pivot freely. On Kato and other engines that do not have telescoping shafts, check that the universal joints slide freely and the "ball and peg" end of the shaft rotates freely. If you notice problems, check for flash or debris on the ends. When you're satisfied with these parts, set them aside for later reassembly.

Truck disassembly also varies on some models. On Athearn, Proto 2000, and some others, the truck sideframes pry off easily. To split the trucks, remove the gearbox clips that are located on both the top and bottom. With the clips off, remove the axles and open up the truck halves to reveal the spur gears. To remove the truck sideframes on Kato and Atlas units you must remove the gear box cover by prying the mounting tabs from the top. When the cover is removed the trucks sideframes come loose. Pull the wheel wipers off the axles so the wheels come free. Separate the truck halves to expose the spur gears. You can leave the motor on the chassis.

Cleaning the drive train. The first order of business is to wash all the lubricant from all drive train components, including the wheels which you haven't removed from the plastic drive gear. Clean with a solution of warm water and a household cleaning solution. For stubborn grease or lubricant use rubbing alcohol. Rinse all parts under hot water and set then aside to dry.

When the parts are dry check them for problems. First check the wheel assemblies for proper gauge with your NMRA gauge. If you find a discrepancy, gently twist the wheel assemblies either in or out depending on the correction needed. Make sure the plastic drive gear remains centered to avoid any problems later. To cut down the chances of an axle assembly being knocked out of gauge, place a small drop of CA or super glue on both sides of the plastic drive gear where the metal wheel stub shaft enters. Now roll the axle assemblies on a flat surface to check for any wobble. If it wobbles, pull the wheels from the center drive gear and check inside the gear for flash and reinstall the wheels. If the problem persists, remove the wheels again and chuck them into a drill. Run the drill at slow-to-medium speed and check for wobble. If the wobble occurs, the problem is in the wheel or stub shaft. If the locomotive is new, check with your dealer for a possible replacement. Replacement wheels are available from several companies and their installation is discussed later. If the wheels run true, then the problem is likely in the drive gear and it should be replaced. When the wheels roll true, set them aside.

Now check for misformed teeth on the wheel and truck spur gears. A more common problem is finding casting flash on the gear sides or edges (photo 2-4) of the center mounting hole. If you find any, trim it away with a sharp no. 11 blade. Even if the flash isn't causing problems now, a piece could break loose later and end up in the gear teeth. After you check the spur gears return them to their mounting shafts on the truck. Turn the gear train with your finger and check for binding. If none is noted add the wheel-axle combinations and replace the gearbox cover and any other gearbox clips. Now roll the truck on a flat surface or piece of track and again check for binding. If everything rolls freely, set the chassis frame back on the trucks. On many units the chassis bolster rests on a metal contact plate. This contact plate is sometimes not square with the truck. If you notice any upward or downward bend, correct it by gently bending it in the proper direction. If these contact plates are not level, the unit may not sit level but may tilt rather unprototypically to one side.

One other area of concern is slack between the worm gear and the bearings at each end. While there is slack between these parts on all locomotives, the problem is more noticeable on

2-5. Under certain operating condition, some Athearn units will surge. If you can't find problems with any other drive-train parts, the culprit may be a slight amount of slack in the worm-gear mounting. Close this gap (at the tip of the knife blade) with a thin washer.

some units when it is not pulling or being pushed by either its own weight or that of a train. At this point the locomotive may start to "buck." It seems that the slack between the worm and bearings (photo 2-5) allows sufficient play to cause this. Inserting thin washers to reduce this space eliminates the problem. It may be difficult to find such thin washers, but you can make this component from thin brass sheets. Drill out the center hole to fit the shaft and use scissors to cut out a small disk. It doesn't have to look perfect—just fill the gap. Do not make the fit so tight that the worm binds. You should still be able to slip a sheet of typing paper between the bearing and worm.

After the entire drive train has been checked and problems corrected, there is one more thing you can do before you lubricate and return the unit to the layout. As mentioned before, the more you run a unit, the better its performance will become. Slight gear wear will produce smoother operation. There is a simple, easy way to accelerate this wear. A tooth polish called Pearl Drops contains a very mild abrasive. Lubricate the truck gears with Pearl Drops and run the unit as if it were a normal break-in. The abrasive action will have the effect of many hours of running with regular lubrication. If you do this, apply a small amount of the polish to the gear teeth and the gear shafts, assemble the chassis, and

run the unit for several hours. Then tear the unit down again and wash off all traces of the polish and set it aside to dry. After everything is dry, lubricate and reassemble the mechanism.

Lubrication. The key to proper lubrication is a matter of choosing the proper lubricant and knowing where to put it. I prefer Labelle lubricants, as they have a complete line including plastic-compatible products. For metal-to-metal bearings such as motor shaft, worm gear, and axle shaft bearings I use Labelle 108, a plastic-compatible light oil. For the worm and spur gears a light coat of Labelle 106 plastic-compatible grease with Teflon is my choice.

To lubricate a unit you must remove the body shell. With the chassis sitting upright, remove the worm gear covers. Apply a small drop of 108 oil to the motor and worm gear bearings in the locations shown. Replace the worm gear covers and remove the bottom gearbox cover to reveal the axle bearings and spur gears. Apply a small drop of 108 to the axle bearings. Now apply Labelle 106 grease to the spur gear teeth. A small dab on a few teeth is all you need. When you run the locomotive the grease will transfer itself evenly to all spur gears and the worm gear. Be sure to wipe off any excess lubricant to prevent dirt build-up. Replace the covers.

Frequency of lubrication is a function of use or lack of use. For most modelers annual lubrication is more

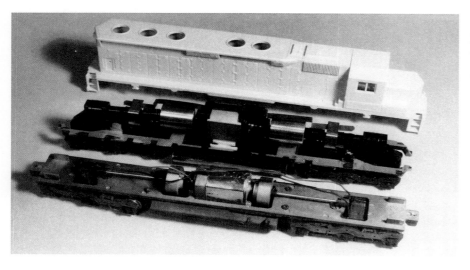

2-6. There are often options when repowering a locomotive or powering a shell. A Rail Power SD45 shell has the two options shown. The top unit is a modified Athearn SD45 chassis, while the bottom drive is an Overland chassis.

2-7. Replace the sintered-iron Athearn wheels with new nickel-silver wheels. They are the correct shape and will stay cleaner than the Athearn wheels.

than adequate. Those who run their locomotives often need to lubricate more frequently. If in doubt, remove the worm gear or bottom gearbox cover and check for lubricant. Some grease should be visible on the spur gears, while a little oil should be noticeable around the shaft and axle bearings. Experience will help you determine lubrication needs more than any maintenance schedule.

REPAIR

Today's better-quality locomotives are nearly trouble free. Given reasonable care, including lubrication and occasional cleaning, they will last for many years. More damage occurs from outside sources than internal problems. Improper or careless handling are most often responsible for any problems that arise. Should any parts break or get damaged you can usually replace them easily. Most manufacturers maintain an extensive parts inventory. Well-stocked hobby shops may also have some of the most common parts in stock or can get them for you. While not of primary concern, it is a good idea to save the parts lists from your locomotives. This will be a handy resource if you ever need to replace damaged parts.

UPGRADING MECHANISMS

If you want the benefits of upgraded mechanisms but don't want the hassle of doing all the work, there are several choices available to you. Some manufacturers such as Proto Power West take an Athearn chassis, add additional weight, a new can motor and flywheels, and tune the chassis as previously described. The result is a flawless piece of railroad power equal to the best. The only thing you need to do is mount the body to the chassis. Several examples are covered in the next chapter.

Overland, the brass importer, offers an extensive line of can-motor-powered chassis. This is a quiet, powerful, and extremely smooth-running chassis equal to the best. As an added bonus, the Overland chassis has an extremely low profile. This feature lets you install a complete cab or some rear engineroom detail without interference from the drive components.

Wheel replacement. While there is nothing seriously wrong with most factory-installed wheels, some companies, such as Jay-Bee and North West Short Line, offer replacement wheels that are nickel-silver plated and accurate in shape. The nickel-silver plating provides a very smooth, hard surface that

does not pick up dirt as readily as the original wheels, while the accurate shape virtually guarantees no wheel wobble. The wheels cost about $1 per axle but the investment will pay for itself in less wheel cleaning and smoother operation.

To replace the wheels, pull the old wheels from the drive gear and replace them with the new wheels, taking care to center the drive gear and accurately regauge the wheels (photo 2-7). Be careful not to damage or bend the plastic drive gear.

WHEEL CLEANING

The most expensive, best-running locomotives built will run up to their potential only if they receive periodic maintenance. The maintenance required most frequently is wheel cleaning (photo 2-8). Location, environment, and frequency of use will determine how often you need to clean them. A good track cleaning program will go a long way toward reducing cleanings, but you will eventually have to do it. There are a number of methods of cleaning wheels, and all are effective.

One method is to scrape the dirt from the wheels with the tip of a knife or with a Moto-tool and a small wire brush. This works well, except that the entire wheel is not accessible. You have to turn the wheels slightly several times to expose the entire wheel. This

2-8. Dirty locomotive wheels will cause operational problems. Early signs of dirt include headlight flicker and some slight hesitation in locomotive operation. If they're not cleaned, performance will degrade until the locomotive hesitates and stalls repeatedly.

2-9. One way to clean wheels is to run the locomotive over a piece of paper towel. Soak the end with a little WD 40 and run the locomotive onto the paper towel repeatedly. You can see the dirt that has been removed. When the dirt is gone, run the locomotive over a dry section of the towel to remove any remaining WD 40. This method requires a minimum of handling and can be done in a minute or two.

method requires a lot of handling that can damage small parts.

Kadee makes a wheel cleaner. To use it, hook two electrical leads to your power pack and open the throttle some. Hook the electrical leads to two electrically separate small wire brushes. When touching the wire brushes to the wheels of an individual axle, power flows through the wheels as if the locomotive were on powered track. Now brush the spinning wheels clean.

I use WD-40 to remove the dirt. I have a short length of flextrack nailed to a board. I hook wire leads to a power pack with alligator clips and open the throttle about one-fourth of the way. I spray a small section of paper towel with WD-40. I lay this wet section across the track with a dry section beyond. Be sure the section of towel between the rails is pushed down slightly so the coupler trip pin does not catch it. I set the locomotive on the rails. The power to the rails causes the locomotive to move down the track and up and onto the WD-40 soaked towel. When the entire locomotive is on the towel or contact is lost I pull the locomotive back onto the bare track and the power again causes it to run onto the towel. After a trip or two the WD-40 softens the dirt and it is deposited on the towel (photo 2-9). Move the towel slightly to run over fresh WD-40. When the wheels no

longer leave dirt on the towel, move a dry section of towel to the rails and run the locomotive on it several times to dry the wheels. Wipe the dirt off the rails and grab the next locomotive. The wheels are now clean with a minimum of handling. After you become proficient at it, you can clean a locomotive's wheels in less than a few minutes.

Other routine maintenance involves periodic lubrication and checking wheel gauge, coupler height, and operation, all of which were discussed earlier. Another operation, although not discussed in the context of maintenance, is the complete tearing down of a chassis. This need not be done often, but if you have a locomotive that just doesn't seem to perform as well as it used to, the problem may be an accumulation of dirt and old lubricant in the drive train. Clean all parts as described previously and re-lubricate. The results may be surprising.

NOISE REDUCTION

While prototype locomotives should emit a certain amount of noise, some locomotives are noisy to the point of being irritating. Unlike the prototype, whose engine and fans are the source of most of the racket, the main culprit on model locomotives is gear noise, which is not music to even a model railroader's ears. Most ready-to-run units are very quiet, and if there is

any significant noise it is usually at higher speeds. I have tried several ways to reduce the noise. The easiest and most effective method is to stuff several small pieces of foam rubber into the upper part of the locomotive body (photo 2-10). You can even use the foam packing in an Athearn locomotive box. Trim several pieces to fit snugly into the shell. The foam will hold itself in place and can be removed easily. The main concern is that it not interfere with the drive train. This method will typically work on any unit as long as there is room inside the body.

2-10. Gear noise in some locomotives can be quite loud. An easy way to reduce the noise is to install several small pieces of foam rubber into the hood. Just be sure the foam rubber does not interfere with any moving parts.

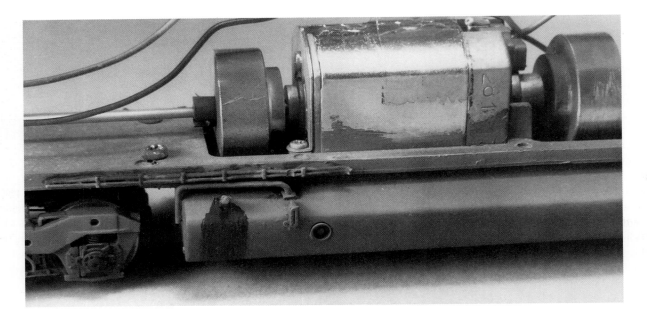

This is a fuel tank of an Overland SD45 repower chassis. The Overland fuel filler and oval sight glass gauge were not up to current standards, so they were replaced with Detail Associates parts. A vent pipe, in-tank gauge, and traction motor cables were also added to this chassis.

3 Underframes

Until now I have covered general information about the hobby and the mechanical side of model locomotives. Now you're ready for some actual detailing.

Prototype chassis have several main components that are virtually universal in location. There is a truck to transfer power to the rails located at each end of the locomotive, and the fuel tank is located between the trucks. A frame keeps the trucks in position, supports the fuel tank, and provides a platform on which to build the rest of the locomotive—a very basic and simple arrangement. Other prototype details in this area include air tanks on most units, and a wide variety of electrical cables and piping for the various locomotive functions.

BODY MOUNTING

A primary consideration with model locomotives is how the underframe attaches to the body. All manufacturers provide a means of attaching these assemblies together. The most common method is to provide mounting tabs that extend down from the body and clip onto the underframe. While most of these mounts are quite effective, on some models it is difficult to separate the body from the underframe. Having to heavy-handedly squeeze the narrow hood of a locomotive shell while pulling on the fuel tank is not my idea of a good time, especially if the models have added detail. One way to lessen the grip of the mounting lugs is to trim a little off the edges of the lugs. The lugs still do a good job of

holding on to the underframe but will dislodge more easily. Some locomotives have mounting tabs that extend down into the frame on both sides just above the trucks. Insert a small screwdriver between the truck and frame and prod a little to work these tabs loose so you can lift the body from the frame.

There is yet another system found on older Athearn locomotives. Body-mounting tabs extend down the outside of the body frame. These tabs have an indentation molded into the back side. The metal underframe of these models have corresponding cast-on pins that fit into the indentations and hold the body in place when the body is positioned over the underframe. While this system works just fine, the body tabs are not prototypical. Even where the tabs are discretely located, the idea of prying under them with a small screwdriver on an exposed area is not desirable. A slip of the screwdriver could put a nasty scratch on a model.

If the unprototypical tabs are bothersome, they could be trimmed off flush along the bottom of the plastic frame. This then leaves the body loose on the chassis. While I'm sure that many modelers run their locomotives like this, I prefer a solid attachment between these two components. Screws provide an easy-to-remove option for attaching the body to the frame. Several options are available here, depending on whether you want the screws out of view or don't mind the heads being visible on the walkways. Leaving them in view offers the easiest solution. I prefer four screws, although two will do in a pinch.

In the illustrated example, I mounted an HO scale Rail Power SD45 shell to a modified Athearn SD45 chassis using four flat-head 0-80 screws. All four screws are located on the long hood walkway. Mark holes on each side of the chassis so they will be located near the rear of the unit and just behind the cab when the body is set on the chassis. Drill a no. 56 hole at each location and use a 0-80 tap to cut the threads. When you've finished tapping the holes, set the body on the chassis and mark the location of the holes on the bottom of the walkway area. Before marking the holes on the left side, install spacers in the raised walkway area. One-inch pieces of Evergreen .100" x .188" strip make ideal spacers. Cement spacers to the bottom of the walkway so they line up with the chassis mounting holes. When the liquid cement has set, mark these holes. Drill the holes through the walkway with a no. 51 bit to clear the 0-80 screws (photo 3-1). Use a 1/8" bit or larger to countersink the screw holes on the top of the walkway (photo 3-2). Be careful not to go too deep, so the screws are flush with the top of the walkway. When the holes are finished, set the body on the chassis. Use 3/16" 0-80 screws on the right side and 3/8" screws

3-1. Two body and two frame holes are visible on this Rail Power SD45 chassis. In this application, install the screws on the top of the walkway and tap them into the frame.

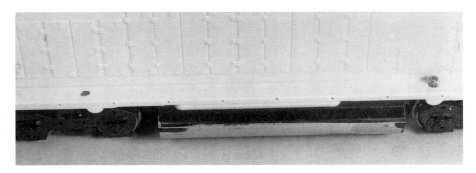

3-2. Another type of screw mounting will leave the screw heads visible. In this case countersink the screws into the tops of the walkways. The screws anchor into drilled and tapped holes in the frame.

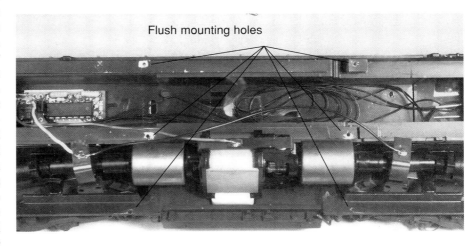

3-3. Mounting a body to a new chassis can get quite involved. The example shown is a Rail Power C30-7 shell that will be mounted on an Athearn U30C chassis with screws. To do it, drill and countersink four screw holes into the bottom of the frame. The screws will anchor into holes drilled and tapped into the walkway and built-up pads under the battery box area.

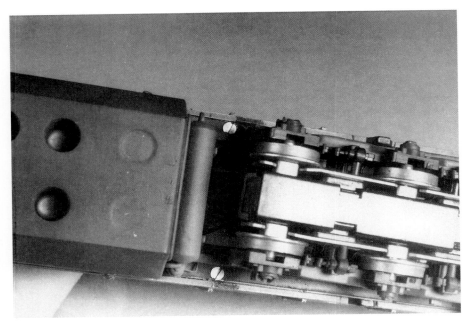

3-4. Two of the four mounting screws are visible in this underside photo of a Rail Power C30-7. The underside mount produces the least visible mounting, as only the ends of the screws are visible on the top of the walkway surfaces. File the ends flush with the surface, and they will be nearly invisible when painted.

sides of the walkway should be built up. Otherwise the top of the fuel tank will be unprototypically close to the bottom of the sidesill. Cement a strip of .040 styrene sheet along the entire length of the bottom of the walkway. Fill the raised battery box section of the walkway, where the front mounting screws are located, with pieces of styrene sheet until they match the height of the lower walkway. Now set the body on the frame and mark the hole locations on the bottom of the walkway. Drill the holes with a no. 56 bit and tap it for 0-80 screws. It can be a challenge to tap the screw threads into the thin styrene walkway. Be careful not to overtighten the screws and strip the threads.

Some of the mounting screws may pass up through the walkway. Trim the screws so they are flush with the top of the walkway when they are fully screwed in. After painting the model, touch up the exposed screw ends with the walkway color to render them nearly invisible.

COUPLER MOUNTING

There are two ways to mount couplers—body mount and underframe mount. The underframe mounting pad on many diesels is designed to accept a snap-on cover holding the supplied hook-horn coupler. Anyone contemplating serious model railroading will soon discard these couplers and

on the left side. If you do a careful job of marking and drilling, the walkway holes should line up perfectly with the holes in the chassis.

The same method will work with other underframes and a variety of shells. Photo 3-3 shows the bottom of an HO scale Rail Power C30-7 shell that is drilled to mount on an Athearn U30-C frame. In this case I preferred to

have the screws less visible, so the flat-headed screws were mounted from the bottom. The location of the holes here is more critical. The screw heads must be accessible from the bottom. The only location where this is possible is between the trucks and the fuel tank (photo 3-4).

Before drilling the no. 51 holes into the bottom of the frame, the under-

3-5. The Athearn coupler mount can be modified to accept Kadee couplers. File the top of the mounting pad flat. Then drill a hole and tap it for a 2-56 screw.

3-6. Use a long-shank coupler so the coupler extends beyond a snowplow. The most important consideration is that the coupler be the proper height. This can be accomplished in one of two ways. Either file the coupler mounting until the coupler height is correct or use a Kadee offset shank coupler to compensate for any differences.

upgrade to Kadee-style couplers. These mounting pads need some attention with a file and must be drilled and tapped to accept any other type of coupler. Photo 3-5 and 3-6 illustrate this modification on an HO scale GP7 underframe.

This modification is necessary on some locomotives because they come equipped with underframe-mounted couplers. On some models these pads are drilled and tapped and include mounting screws. They are the perfect height for the "standard" Kadee no. 5 coupler.

Couplers can also be mounted directly to the locomotive body. Specific instructions on the process are included in Chapter 5, Bodies.

FUEL TANKS

Fuel tanks are one of those details that seem simple and unassuming at first glance but appear quite intricate upon close inspection. Obviously not all fuel tanks are the same, and different railroads sometimes specified different-size tanks for various reasons.

Model locomotives have a somewhat "standard" fuel tank for the particular model of the prototype locomotive they represent. This is simple economics, as the manufacturers want their product to appeal to as large a group as possible. If the locomotive you are modeling has a different configuration, then it is up to you to either ignore it or change it. Because a fuel tank is such a large item, ignoring a major difference would be detrimental to the finished model. Changing a fuel tank to match a specific prototype can set the model apart from a host of other locomotives whose modelers ignored the difference.

Several examples of fuel tank modifications are given in this chapter. While in each case the exact prototype tank length is not known, by using various prototype features as benchmarks you can determine the length of the tank and modify the model accordingly. **Shortening the fuel tank.** Milwaukee Road GP38-2 number 350 is an Athearn unit. The fuel tank was short-

3-7. This is a drastically shortened Athearn tank on a Milwaukee Road GP38-2. Part of the fuel tank must remain to avoid seriously weakening the frame. A nonstandard fuel filler is located just in front of the tank.

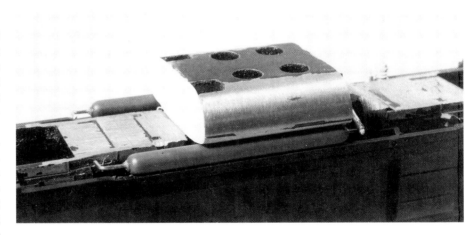

3-8. The thin styrene sheet cemented to the back of the tank covers the exposed body-mounting lug openings. Note that the front lug openings are already gone. This is also an excellent view of the new air tanks added to the body.

ened on both ends to match the prototype. The drastic shortening needed in this case could have compromised the structural integrity of the frame. To avoid weakening the frame any more than necessary, not all material was removed from the front of the tank. Another problem was that two of the four body-mounting lugs were completely removed and a portion of the other two were removed as well. Concerns about holding the body to the underframe were unfounded, as the remaining lugs adequately held the body into place.

To begin shortening the tank, remove all parts from the underframe. Mark the tank to show the cut lines. Clamp the frame in a vise and use a hacksaw to remove the unneeded tank ends. Don't cut on the line, but about 1/16" back so you can remove saw marks with a large mill file. Remove the rear of the tank completely with two cuts—one from the bottom of the tank up to the bottom of the frame, and the other from the back of the tank flush with the bottom of the frame to meet the first cut. Cut the front of the tank up to 1/8" from the bottom of the frame. Remove

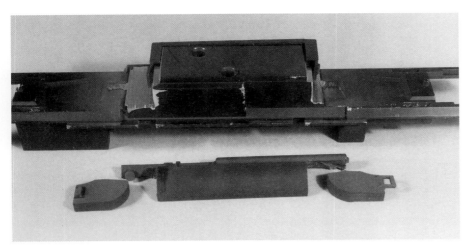

3-9. A Kato fuel tank can also be shortened. To shorten this SD40 tank remove some length from each end of the plastic tank sides. Then cement the ends to the remaining tank body. Also shorten the metal underframe portion of the tank so the tank sides will fit again.

3-10. Lengthen a fuel tank by cementing styrene sheets to the end of the tank. When it's the proper length, use a file to remove excess styrene, matching the existing tank contours. Fill the notch in this particular tank with styrene strips epoxied into place and finish it to match the tank contours. Fill any gaps with thickened CA or body putty and finish when dry.

3-8). Remove the front mounting lugs from the GP38-2 body and trim the rear of the back mounting lugs until they fit the narrowed notches. The tank modification is now complete and ready for further detailing.

Some manufacturers' locomotives have plastic fuel tanks that fit over a metal frame. These can be shortened but will require shortening both the plastic tank and the metal part of the frame to which the tank attaches. The example shown is a Kato SD40 tank shortened to a scale 3 feet 9 inches. You'll need to remove material from both the front and rear of the tank—3 feet off the back and 9 inches off the front. Photo 3-9 shows the tank in pieces awaiting reassembly and the metal underframe trimmed for reinstallation. Do the plastic work first, cement the parts together, and fill any gaps. Remove the same amount of material from the metal tank casting as you removed from each end of the plastic tank. File the notches back in the bottom edges so the tank sits properly.

Lengthening the fuel tank. The frame under my heavily kitbashed Santa Fe SD26 4613 came from an Athearn SD7. I lengthened the tank and filled in the notch in the tank. Start the project by removing all parts from the frame. Fill the notch with pieces of .06 styrene cut to extend beyond the outside edge of the tank. Attach these pieces with Super Jet CA. Lengthen the front of the tank with four pieces of .04 styrene sheet cut slightly larger than the tank. Square up the front of the fuel tank with a large mill file so the added styrene lies flat. Attach the first piece with Super Jet and let it set before attaching the three remaining pieces with liquid cement. When everything has set hard, use a large mill file to remove the excess styrene using the existing contours of the tank as a guide. Continue with the mill file into the metal tank sides until you remove all low spots and blemishes. Be careful to maintain the rounded tank contours. Use the file on the back surface of the tank to smooth and square it up also. Check the metal-styrene joints for any gaps and seams. If

the two sides by sawing parallel to the side of the frame up to the first cut. Remove the remaining middle of the tank's front by sawing parallel with the bottom of the frame up to the first cut.

Finish the tank ends with a large mill file up to the marked locations. Make sure the ends are square.

Using the file, finish the front portion that was left for additional strength to the shape shown (photo 3-7). There is usually a seam on the side of the Athearn tanks. Remove it using

the large mill file, taking care to keep the round contour of the EMD tank. Finish the front of the tank except for final smoothing with very fine emery paper. The mounting lug notches on the rear of the tank are exposed. To cover these, use a .010 piece of Evergreen styrene cut a little larger than the rear of the tank, cementing it in place with Slow Jet CA. When the cement has set, trim the overhanging edges with a sharp knife and finish the entire tank with very fine emery paper (photo you find any, fill them with Super Jet. When the CA has set sufficiently, smooth the area with the mill file again. If any gaps remain, repeat the process until the all blemishes are gone. When filling is complete, finish the tank sides and ends with very fine emery cloth to achieve a smooth finish (photo 3-10).

Cleaning up the metal tank casting. The most common flaw in model fuel tanks is the presence of casting seams. Use a large mill file to smooth the seam and any other rough areas while retaining the existing tank contour. While you're at it, remove the lumps that are supposed to represent the fuel filler and gauge (photo 3-11). Replace these with separate detail parts. If some depressions are too deep to file out, fill them with Slow Jet and finish the areas when the CA has set. Athearn's GE fuel tanks also have a few rough spots on their sides. Attention with a large mill file will correct these problems. This will remove the cast-on fuel gauge detail but you can replace it later. While in the area with the file, give the lower, angled sides of the fuel tank some attention. File until the resulting flat area extends all the way out to the side of the tank. This little extra will give the tank nice prototypically sharp corners (photo 3-12).

Sometimes a tank is not properly shaped. Rather than discard it, you can reshape it to a more accurate profile. This is the case with the plastic fuel tank found on the Smokey Valley GP15-1. The top angled surface is too steep, giving the tank a thin appearance from the side. Photo 3-13 shows the right side of the tank with a base piece of .08 styrene topped with a piece of .04 styrene. Use liquid cement to secure them. Use a large mill file to reshape the tank with the left side of the tank showing the results.

Using these examples and your own ingenuity, you should be able to modify just about any tank to any configuration you need.

Tank lip. On some EMD prototype units there is a distinct lip on both the front and rear of the fuel tank. While this detail does not exist on all units, it is a neat item to model on units where

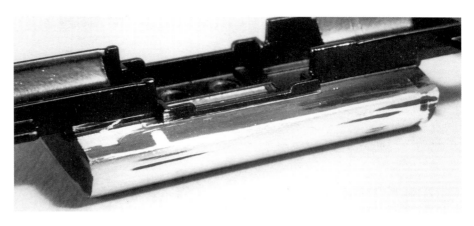

3-11. Smooth casting lines on the Athearn fuel tank should be worked with a large mill file. If you're replacing cast-on tank details with more accurate parts, cut the old parts off with a razor saw and smooth the area with a file. Use progressively finer grades of emery cloth to remove any file marks.

3-12. Smooth the sides of an Athearn GE fuel tank with a large mill file to remove any casting flash and rough spots. The corners will benefit from the filing, as they will be nice and sharp-looking like the prototype. Replace the cast-on fuel gauges with the face of a modified Detail Associates gauge from their fuel tank fittings set.

it exists. To model the lip, first use a large mill file to smooth both the front and rear of the fuel tank. Then cut two pieces of .010 styrene sheet slightly larger than the tank ends and use either CA or 5-minute epoxy to secure them to the ends. When the adhesive has set, trim the lip to a uniform height. Do this using a small piece of .010 styrene sheet as a guide. Slide this guide along the tank next to the lip while using a knife or file to remove the material extending beyond the thickness of the guide. When the excess material has been removed, finish the edge with very fine sandpaper to remove any rough or "fuzzy" edges. Photo 3-14 shows an Athearn GP40-2 tank with a .010 lip added.

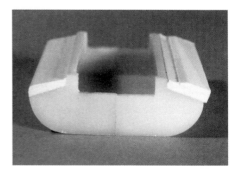

3-13. A poorly shaped plastic tank can be made more accurate by cementing styrene pieces to the tank and finishing them to match a more accurate tank contour. This tank is from a Smokey Valley GP15-1 kit. The top of the tank has too much slope. Cement styrene strips to the top of the tank and file them to shape when dry.

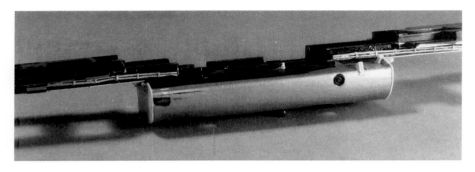

3-14. A detailed Athearn GP40-2 frame is ready for painting. Here you can see the standard fuel tank fittings. Install the extended front and rear edges and Detail Associates traction motor cables along the frame edges.

3-15. This is a fuel tank from an Athearn SD40-2 with new fuel filler, fuel gauges, and vent pipe added.

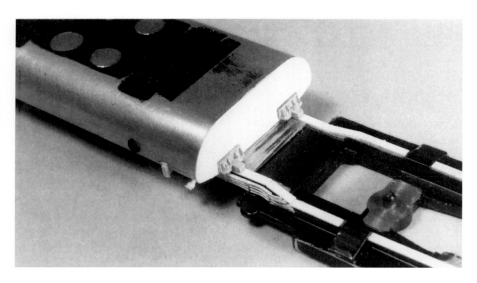

3-16. This bottom view of the GP40-2 frame shows the extended tank edge, fuel tank mounting brackets, traction motor cables, and the pieces of 1 x 6 Evergreen styrene strip representing the bottom web of the prototype frame.

Fuel fillers. Fuel tanks have several interesting details that are easily modeled with readily available detail parts. To locate these details accurately, good prototype information is a must, as some railroads use different or multiple fillers and gauges and some are in non-standard locations. As a general rule, the fuel fillers are located near the front of the tanks on EMD prototypes. The fuel fillers of GE prototype units are located either at the ends or near the center of the tank. Often these units appear to have fuel fillers at both ends of the tank. This may be true but it is likely that one of the fillers, usually the rear, is a dummy and not used. There are several types of end caps, depending of the railroad's refueling system, and several different caps are included in the Detail Associates set (photo 3-15).

Fuel gauges. There are several types of fuel gauge. What's called a vertical sight glass is present on nearly all diesels. This gauge is self-explanatory, as it has a long vertical shape. On all EMD prototype units these are located slightly behind the fuel filler along the top edge of the fuel tank. On GE prototypes they are located below the fuel fillers. On units with dummy fillers, there is a dummy gauge as well. On Alco and MLW units these gauges are also located near the fuel fillers.

Some EMD and GE prototypes have an in-tank dial gauge. These are circular in shape and are located on the sides of the tank also near the fuel filler. Not all units have them and, more confusing yet, some only have them on one side. Prototype photos are a must to determine your railroad's preferences.

Another type is the top-mount dial gauge. These are located on the top of the tanks near the fillers. This type of gauge is on newer units, although not universally. The EMD gauge looks like a meat thermometer sticking out of the tank, while the GE gauge is in a circular housing. Units with top-mounted dial gauges do not have in-tank dial gauges.

Vent pipe. The fuel tank vent pipe is another added detail. While vent pipes are not visible on GE locomotives, they are visible on the front left side of second-generation EMD units. The vent pipe is attached to the tank right behind the vertical sight glass on the left side. It makes an upside-down "U" and ends at the bottom of the tank. Several mounting straps hold the pipe to the front of the tank. Detail Associates .022 brass wire works well for modeling this detail.

Tank brackets. While this particular detail is nearly invisible under the frame, adding a set of Detail Associates EMD tank brackets to the junction of the fuel tank and frame is a nice little detail. While Detail Associates casts these brackets as pairs connected with a thin spacer, it works best if you remove the spacers and attach each bracket separately to the tank. Thickened CA works well for installing these parts. Photo 3-16 shows a set of tank brackets installed.

MISCELLANEOUS DETAILS

Several miscellaneous details unrelated to the tank or fuel supply are sometimes attached to the tank. Sometimes there are vent pipes or a small waste tank attached to the back of the fuel tank. Before the current heightened environmental awareness, most waste from the engine room was allowed to fall on the right-of-way. Now these wastes are collected into a holding tank and are treated at engine facilities. A photo of a vent or tank is a necessity for any type of accurate modeling.

Some railroads locate spare coupler knuckle brackets on the top of the fuel tank on both GE and EMD prototype units. Again, check prototype photos for accurate placement. There are many more details located in these areas, so be sure to check your prototype photos for additional information.

SIDESILL-WALKWAYS

The sidesill-walkway area is unique to the road switcher and switcher models, as it provides an access area around the locomotive. Model manufacturers have several ways of dealing with these areas. On many one-piece shells this area is molded with the body. On some units this area is molded as a separate part.

3-17. The air tank pipe, air filter, bell, and fuel tank fittings on this Athearn U30C frame detailed for a C30-7 Rail Power body are all new detail parts.

3-18. This is how it looks after it's been painted and the body has been installed. Mount spare coupler knuckles on top of the fuel tank to the left of the fuel fittings.

While casting this as a separate part from the rest of the body is not a major deal, it does give you easier access to some areas for detailing.

This area does not need a lot of modifications. Prototype locomotives have a raised tread pattern on the walkway areas to prevent slipping. On some models this tread pattern is represented. For modelers wishing to add this detail on units not so equipped, Precision Investment Associates makes an etched-brass walkway tread kit for the HO scale SD40-2. Because of the SD40-2's large size, the kit has large pieces of tread that can be cut up and used on a variety of units. Use sharp scissors to cut the pieces and secure them with thickened CA.

A frame modification unique to later model EMDs built after 1983 involves the sidesills. Pre-1983 units have a stepped sidesill. This is the type represented on most Athearn model road switchers. After 1983, however, EMD built all subsequent GP38-2, 39, 40-2, 49, 50 and SD40-2s with the straight sill. This detail change can easily be modeled by removing the lower portion of the sidesill step. The only area this will affect is around the jacking pads, which will become slightly

4256

3-19. The Atlas model of the C425 is a Phase I unit with an air tank on each side of the unit. To model a Phase 2 unit, mount both air tanks on the right side of the unit. Move the air tanks from their positions and mount them on the right side of the unit. Connect the two tanks with a short piece of .022 brass wire and leave the cast-on pipes at the tank ends as is.

low. A large file will work well for removing the extra material. Just be sure to keep the sill straight.

AIR TANKS

Air tanks on prototype locomotives are usually mounted near the fuel tanks. On EMD road switchers, they are located between the walkway and the top of the fuel tank, with a few exceptions that were roof-mounted or mounted crosswise behind the fuel tank. The only standard roof-mounted

tanks were on the EMD SD24. A few GPs and GP GP35s had roof-mounted tanks because larger fuel tanks were requested on the units.

Air tanks on GE's prototype U and Dash 7 units are mounted on the front and the rear of the fuel tank. On the Dash 8 and Dash 9 models they are inset on the right side of the fuel tank. Luckily, the model manufacturers do a good job with the basic tank. All you need to do is add the small details and piping. Alcos and most switchers also have side-

mounted tanks. These can be plumbed and detailed as photo 3-19 indicates.

Nearly every model manufacturer handles the air tanks differently. Kato casts their air tanks together with the fuel tank and includes some cast-on piping. Athearn, which has the most extensive line of EMD road switchers, casts theirs with the body. While the Athearn air tanks look passable from the side, any kind of angled view shows them for what they are, a virtual silhouette. This area can be improved easily. Both Details West and Detail Associates offer the 15" tanks needed. The Details West tanks are cast metal with details but are not perfectly round. The Detail Associates 15" tanks are styrene with cast-on mounting bands. I prefer the Detail Associates tanks. File off the mounting band detail and sand it smooth. Drill the ends for .019 brass wire. Slice off the cast-on tanks and mount the new tanks in the same location. Build up the left underside of the frame with scrap styrene so it is up to the proper level before mounting the tank.

AIR FILTERS

Air filters are small details that are almost universally located near the front right side of the fuel tank on road switchers. On some units the filters are hidden behind low skirting. On switchers these filters are usually located below

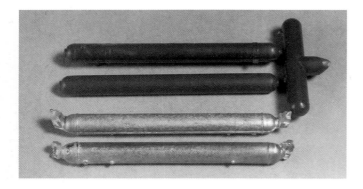

3-20. The upper set of these two sets of 15" air tanks is from Detail Associates. The top tank appears as it was purchased; the bottom tank, with its side details removed, is cleaned up and ready for mounting. The lower tanks are from Details West. The top tank is as bought, complete with casting seams; the bottom tank is cleaned up and ready for mounting.

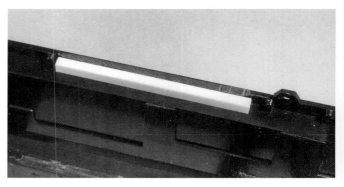

3-21. To mount new air tanks on Athearn EMD units remove the cast-on tanks. Install a piece of .10 x .10 styrene under the left walkway area of the frame to raise this tank to the proper height. Also, bevel the bottom edges of the sidesill so the new air tanks to sit properly under the unit.

the cab on the right side. There are several styles of filters, and the type used depended on the locomotive model and sometimes railroad preference.

Details West has a wide selection of filters, and they have decent instructions for installation. Because these parts are usually located right behind the front truck, you may have to move the filters slightly from exact prototype location to allow the truck to move. For most applications cement the filters to the bottom of the walkway with CA. If the metal underframe interferes with this type of installation, notch it to clear the filters. This is common on Kato units. There are cast dimples on some filters where air lines can be added. If they are to be included, drill the holes before installing the filters. Use prototype photos to plumb the filters (photo 3-23).

FRAME DETAILS

Locomotive frames are largely invisible under the locomotive. This makes observing frame details, various piping, and cables difficult except under certain side light conditions. The same goes for model locomotives. These areas are largely hidden in shadow, and adding these difficult-to-observe details would by most be considered a waste of time. For those willing to go the extra mile in detailing, adding such details can give a model a little extra "wow" when others observe the unit up close.

The locomotive frame's primary support members are steel I-beams. To simulate the web on the model frame, use thin Evergreen strip as shown in photo 3-16. While not completely accurate, it will give the impression of an I-beam.

As for cables, Details West offers a set of traction motor cables that you can attach to the sides of the frame with CA. Use various sizes of wire to simulate different pipes. With several good photos of these areas you can have a field day detailing the frame area. The piping and details you can add to the frame area are only limited by your time and patience.

3-22. Drill the ends of the Detail Associated tanks on a GP38-2 unit with a .022 bit and install similar-sized brass wire as reservoir air lines.

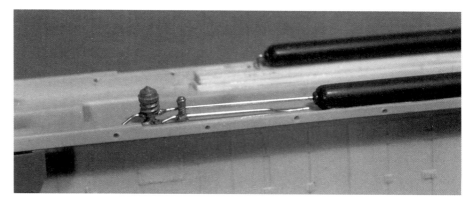

3-23. Install air tanks, air filters, and associated plumbing on this Rail Power SD45 body. While the plumbing may not be totally accurate, it does capture the busy look of the prototype unit in this area.

3-24. New fuel tank and underframe details will give added interest to any unit. Here, fuel fittings, air tanks, air filters, associated wire piping, and traction motor cables have been added to this CNW SD45.

The replacement of the cast-on brake cylinders and the addition of brake cylinder air lines and a speed recorder brings the detail on this Athearn sideframe to the same high level as the rest of this kitbashed ATSF SD26.

4 Truck Sideframes

The plastic truck sideframes, like most parts of model locomotives, are purely cosmetic. All mechanical functions are contained in the body of the truck. The sideframe is attached to this body but has no mechanical function.

There are two basic types of trucks, a two-axle type, known as a B truck, and a three-axle, known as a C truck. Most prototype manufacturers include some type of truck designation in the locomotive name. GE includes either the "C" or "B" in their locomotive designation. Alco denoted axles on early units by using an RS for the two-axle units and RSD for those with three. Their later Century series noted the total axle number as the first digit in the locomotive designation—a C425 used B trucks, while the C636 used C trucks. EMD denoted the difference on road switchers by designating B truck units as GPs and C trucks as SDs. On early cab units, all F units rode on B trucks and E models used C trucks. EMD also had a four-axle or D truck on their DD40AX units built for Union Pacific, but production of these curiosities was limited to these units.

While there are many types of sideframes, they all share the same basic design and many of the same basic details. Sideframe details include journal bearings, a springing or suspension system, sand pipes, brake cylinders, and brake shoes. A number of accessories can also be located on the truck frames, including speed recorders, wheel slip indicators, rerail frogs, and some signal activation equipment.

Detailing model trucks is usually a simple process. Model manufacturers have for the most part given us wonderfully detailed sideframes that only need a few additional detail items to be stunning copies of the real thing. But as in most other areas of this hobby, not all sideframes are high quality and finely detailed, nor are all prototype options offered in model form. With many detail parts available and a variety of sideframes to choose from, you will be able to upgrade and

Most of cylinders removed

4-1. To add SD40 sideframes on a Kato unit, convert the low-mount brake cylinders to high mounts. Removing the low cylinders is quite difficult, as the plastic used on the sideframes is very tough. Using the photo as a guide, remove as much of the cylinders as possible. A no. 17 X-acto blade will work well. Part of the upper half of the cylinder will remain but it will barely be visible under normal viewing conditions.

4-2. Backdating an Athearn HTC sideframe from an SD40-2 to a Flex-i-coil sideframe is easy. The bottom sideframe is the stock Athearn sideframe. To model the middle version, remove the right sideframe extension and drill out the middle journal with a Hyatt roller bearing for a speed recorder. The high-mount air cylinders and the new Hyatt journal have been installed on the completed top sideframe.

properly detail even a poor sideframe.

While you can detail your trucks with a whole host of parts, there are times when all the detail in the world will not change the fact that a truck sideframe may be inaccurate for a particular model. You may be able to correct this inaccuracy with a few small details, or you may need to do extensive work or even replace the locomotive-supplied trucks with a correct set.

The EMD Flex-i-coil truck is rather unique for EMD in that the brake cylinders on early examples are mounted low on the sideframes between the wheels. The Kato SD40 comes with these sideframes. You can add wire piping to these following the example shown. On the prototype these low cylinders were quite vulnerable in even the slightest derailment. Eventually railroads tired of replacing the low cylinders and mounted them near the top of the truck. Usually only the damaged cylinder was replaced, so some locomotives or even an individual truck might have both types. To model this on Kato sideframes, carve as much of the low cylinder away as possible. This is hard, as the Kato sideframes are made from a very tough material. Now add a regular cylinder in the high position and add the wire piping. Photo 4-1 shows a modified Kato sideframe.

When modeling a Conrail SD40-2 I noticed that they were delivered with the older SD40-style Flex-i-coil trucks. Wanting to model the unit as accurately as possible, I looked for solutions. Athearn makes a high-mount Flex-i-coil truck that is used on its SD45. I figured I could just remove the SD40-2s HTC truck frames and replace them with the correct frames. Wrong! They didn't fit. Rather than modify the truck mounting pins, I backdated the HTC truck. Photo 4-2 shows the process and the result. While not totally accurate, it does capture the main spotting features of the Flex-i-coil truck.

Some truck frames have gone through a kind of detail evolution. Such is the case with the EMD Blomberg truck. In its early days, axles rode in babbitt bearing journals and the locomotive was supported by leaf springs. Two brake cylinders came to bear on four cast-iron brake shoes. This is called the Blomberg B truck.

Over the years the basic Blomberg sideframe has stayed the same but some details have changed. Now roller bearings have replaced babbitt journals, a combination of rubber and metal have replaced the leaf springs, and one brake cylinder instead of two provides enough force for the two remaining composite brake shoes that replaced four cast-iron shoes. There is also a snubber installed on the right journal on each sideframe. During the course of this evolution quite a few EMD units were delivered with a combination of the old and new details.

4-3. The sideframe on the right is a detailed Athearn Blomberg M frame. Note the speed recorder drive and the sand pipes. The sideframe on the left is an Athearn Blomberg B frame. Remove the outboard brake shoes from it to make it look more like an M sideframe than a B sideframe. This is a common sideframe on many GP38-2 and 40-2 units.

4-4. These are sideframes from an Athearn SD7 showing the conversion from cast-on brake cylinders to more detailed separate castings. The top sideframe is unmodified. On the middle sideframe remove the cast-on cylinders and drill for the new parts. Install new cylinders on the bottom sideframe.

4-5. To modify Athearn SD7 sideframes for an ATSF SD26, remove and replace the cast-on brake cylinders with separate brake cylinder castings and air lines. Install a speed recorder drive on the top sideframe.

hole through each ear. Photo 4-3 shows a truck modified in this manner.

BRAKE CYLINDERS

Brake cylinders are a major detail on sideframes. For trucks with separate brake cylinders, just drill the end of each cylinder with a no. 80 bit and bend and install some .012 brass wire to represent air lines. If you use Athearn cylinders, there is usually a casting line along the side of the cylinder. Remove this by scraping and sanding. If the cylinders are cast on the sideframes, add wire piping, but if cast-on cylinders bother you, replace them. A no. 17 blade is excellent for removing the cast-on parts. Slice the cylinder castings off flush with the sideframe and smooth the area with a file and sandpaper. Determine the location of the replacement cylinders and mark and drill the holes in the frame. Before mounting the new cylinders, drill them for the wire air lines. Use liquid cement or CA to attach the new cylinders. Photo 4-4 shows a cylinder replacement sequence using Athearn SD7 sideframes and photo 4-5 shows two completed and painted sideframes.

You must determine which if any variations are present and alter the truck details as needed.

BRAKES

When modeling an EMD GP unit using an Athearn model, you have the choice of two excellent Blomberg sideframes, the earlier B and the later M style. The B frames are supplied with their F units, GP7 and GP35, while the more modern GP38-2, 40-2, 50 and 60s come with the M frame. Many prototype GP38-2 and 40-2s were delivered with a slightly modified B frame. The most common modification was the use of two brake shoes instead of four.

Modeling one of these modified B frame units is easy. Replace the Athearn-supplied M frames with B frames and remove the outboard brake shoes. This modification is quite easy. You could merely hack off the outboard brake shoes and call it done. But if you look closely at the top shoe mounting, you find a small mounting "ear" remaining on the prototype. In fact, this "ear" is present on the M sideframe. Then why not just use the M frame that has this detail already modeled and replace the snubber with a Hyatt journal? Observed closely, the M's combination spring doesn't match the B's leaf springs, and changing this detail would be difficult. Remove the brake shoes and carefully trim the top ear to match the ear on the M frame. Complete the job by drilling a no. 80

AIR LINES

Air lines are easy to make and install. To bend air lines for Athearn's Blomberg, late Flex-i-coil, and HTC truck use the photo 4-6 as a guide. A

4-6. To make a simple jig for bending air lines on EMD Blomberg B trucks, space two pieces of $\frac{1}{16}$" tubing $1\frac{3}{8}$" apart. Bend .012 brass wire around the tubing and trim it to fit in the holes previously drilled in the brake cylinders. For EMD Flex-i-coil and HTC trucks space the tubing $2\frac{3}{16}$" apart.

4-7. These are sideframes from an Overland SD45 low-mount brake cylinder chassis. The top sideframe has a .012 air line running from the brake cylinders. The middle sideframe has an ATS pick-up shoe mounted on the right journal. The lower sideframe has a speed recorder drive attached to the middle journal.

small block of wood and several nails or short pieces of ¹⁄₁₆" brass tubing are all you need. Cut four pieces of .012 brass wire and bend them around the jig. Trim the ends so they fit into the cylinders and install them. Secure the ends with a small drop of CA. For air lines on the single cylinder Blomberg M truck use a shorter piece of wire and bend it over one nail and install it.

Early Flex-i-coil trucks with low-mounted brake cylinders also have air lines. The lines drop down from the frame area and bend at the top of the truck, and a line heads to each brake cylinder. Use the photo of a low-mount sideframe as a guide when bending .012 wire to represent the air line. The tee is not necessary, as a line extending up to the frame may interfere with truck movement. Secure the air line to the truck sideframe with CA. Photo 4-7 shows this brake line. The air lines of GE and some MLW units have more of a square bend. Make them in a jig using ⅛" square tubing, or use a ruler to bend them at the proper point.

JOURNALS

The truck journals are cast details on model sideframes and for the most part they are accurate. In cases in which quality is poor and more accurate and detailed versions are available it is not difficult to slice off the old journals and replace them. In some cases, the prototype trucks have been modified or modernized and new journals were installed. Again, if the parts are available it is an easy improvement. Sometimes a loco-

4-8. Of the two modified Athearn Blomberg B sideframes, the one on the left has been back-dated. To do this replace the Hyatt roller bearings with older-style square and sloped journals. Add an air line and a sand pipe on the left side of the right sideframe. Don't add a sand pipe on the right side because it will interfere with the truck's swing past the boarding steps.

motive needs an earlier-equipped version of a truck. Some sideframes like the EMD Blomberg go back to the early days of diesel building, and the journals hark back to the days before roller bearings.

A number of years ago I was preparing to model CNW GP7 number 4326 as it appeared in 1986. Looking closely at the locomotive, I noticed older square and sloped journals instead of the Hyatt roller bearings standard on most units. To model these features I sliced off the Hyatt roller bearings flush with the surface of the pedestal liners. I assembled and attached the new Detail Associates journals with liquid cement. Photo 4-8 shows a truck detailed in this manner. As a side note, I crossed paths with the 4326 several years later and either the journals were replaced with Hyatts or the trucks were replaced—the unit's truck now sports Hyatt journals. Such is the nature of modeling. What is accurate one day may not be the next.

Another type of journal is actually a combination of parts. Some builders add a shock absorber or snubber to the journal of certain current units. The

prototype reasons for these are complicated but for modeling purposes they are easy to add either as a modification or to replace a cast-on part. Athearn SD40-2s HTC trucks and the modern GP series using the Blomberg M truck include excellent add-on parts you can install. Their GE C trucks do not share these separate details but have the snubbers cast on the frame. Detail Associates makes an excellent set of GE snubbers. Use a no. 17 X-acto knife to remove the cast-on snubbers and replace them with the new parts (photo 4-9). The difference is worth the effort.

SPEED RECORDERS

Speed recorders are present in some form or another on every diesel locomotive. While they may not be readily visible on older locomotives, they are quite visible on those built in the last 30 years. They are located on the truck nearest the cab, and their presence is marked by a cable leading from a journal up to the frame.

On some older units the drive head may be built into the journal and only

4-9. Remove the cast-on snubber from the BN C30-7 sideframe and replace it with the new Detail Associates snubber. The parking brake lever and eyebolt are also visible just ahead of the snubber. Make the lever from thin sheet brass for strength.

4-10. This front left sideframe from a Kato GP35 shows the model after installation of a speed recorder drive and a brake air line.

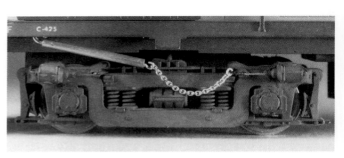

4-11. On the left rear truck of a CN GP40-2W, you can see this Athearn Blomberg M sideframe detailed with sand pipes and an airline. The cable extending from the left journal is a wheel slip indicator. To create this model use a Detail Associates speed recorder base with the drive head hole plugged with styrene. The cable is a piece of .019 brass wire mounted in a similar-size hole in the center of the base.

4-12. To install the parking brake chain and guide pipe on an Atlas C425, attach the pipe (1/16" tube, 11/16" long) to the underside of the frame with a piece of .022 brass wire slid into the pipe and inserted into a hole drilled into the underside of the walkway. The chain is Builders in Scale 40-link-per-inch chain attached to the pipe and brake lever with Detail Associates eyebolts.

the cable is visible. Using a prototype photo as a guide, drill a small hole in the journal and duplicate the cable route with appropriately sized brass wire. Extend the wire up to the frame, but not so high as to interfere with truck motion.

On newer locomotives the drive heads are located on the outside of the journal. These are easily modeled, as Detail Associates offers several excellent parts for both EMD and GE. Use the correct part for your locomotive. Follow the package instructions for drilling the proper size hole in the journal. Secure the drive base with CA. The drive head has a cast-on mounting pin on which to install the cable. This can break off if handled too roughly. If this happens, trim the end off the drive head and drill a no. 80 hole through it. Trim a little in-

sulation from the cable so a short length of wire is visible. Insert it into the hole and secure it with CA. The top of the cable should extend up to just under the frame. Secure the cable to the sideframe with a small drop of CA. This will provide a secure installation (photo 4-10).

On some prototype installations the drive cable is quite a bit smaller than the wire supplied. You can duplicate this by drilling the drive head as before and using the supplied wire with the insulation removed or with small-diameter brass wire that roughly matches the appearance of the prototype.

Some locomotives appear to have more than one speed recorder drive. These extra drives are wheel slip indicators. Generally they are smaller than the speed recorder drives and can be

modeled using the recorder drive head alone drilled into the journal. Use prototype photos to properly model these details where appropriate.

SAND PIPES

Sand pipes are a nice little detail to add if space permits. These pipes can be modeled two ways, with brass wire making a "hard" pipe, or with a thin insulated wire like Detail Associates speed recorder cable, which makes a "soft" flexible pipe. It's important to mount them so they don't interfere with the truck motion in any way.

PARKING BRAKE CHAINS

Parking brake chains are a little different from the average detail part. While they are purely a cosmetic detail,

4-13. This Athearn GE "C" sideframe is detailed for a BN C30-7. To do this, replace the cast-on snubbers with Detail Associated parts. The center journal has a Detail Associates GE speed recorder drive and the right journal has a wheel slip indicator, which is a modified drive head from the GE speed recorder drive. The two parts between the left and center journal are guides for the parking brake chain.

4-14. Install the drive cables and put the handbrake chain in place.

the delicate look of the fine chain hanging below the frame is a stunning detail. Some applications are complicated and may be more grief than the detail is worth. The primary consideration when adding this detail is that you can remove one end of the chain when the body is separated from the chassis. Detail Associated wire eyebolts can do this.

The simplest installations are on GE and some Alco B truck locomotives. The CNW C425 illustrates such an application. This Atlas C425 did not have the guide pipe, so you will have to make one from 1/16" brass tubing. CA a wire eyebolt to the end with the eye slightly opened. Attach a wire eyebolt to the brake cylinder actuating arm in front of the rear cylinder with the eye also slightly opened. Hang the end links of the chain on the open eyes. The length of the Builders in Scale chain is determined by the truck motion. When the truck is fully turned away from the guide pipe, the chain should still have a little slack. With the eyes opened you can unhook at least one end of the chain when you remove the body from the chassis (photo 4-12).

This installation is more complicated on a BN C30-7. While simple in the fact that the chain still goes from the guide pipe, to a brake shoe actuating lever, you must thread it through two truck-mounted guides. Photo 4-13 shows the brackets installed and photo 4-14 shows the completed installation. The truck guides on this model are fabricated from brass and attached with CA. Figure 1 shows the dimensions and locations of these parts. The chain can be left loose in the guides or can be glued with CA inside the guides to create the proper sag.

RERAIL FROGS

Rerail frogs are carried on some locomotives. Most are located near the truck area, as that is where they will likely be used. In other instances, they are carried in the frame area. On some units, CN hung the rerail frogs from the frame right alongside the front right and left rear trucks (see photo 4-11). Install opened Detail Associates eyebolts or

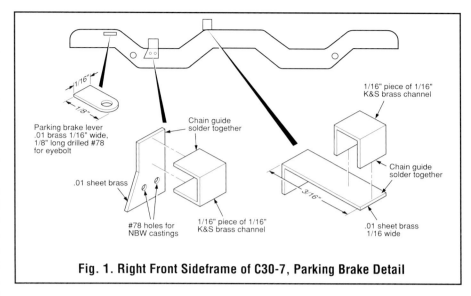

Fig. 1. Right Front Sideframe of C30-7, Parking Brake Detail

4-15. Here is a close-up of a Flex-i-coil sideframe detailed with an air line going to the low-mounted brake cylinders and an ATS shoe mounted on the front journal.

hooks fashioned from .012 brass wire under the locomotive sidesills and hang the rerail frogs from them. Some railroads conveniently locate mounting frogs right on the trucks. Soo Line did this on some early SD40-2s. To model such a detail, use Detail Associates' flat brass wire to make simple hooks and attach them to the truck with CA. Glue the frog with CA into the hooks and the truck sideframe for a strong installation. Refer to prototype photos when adding such detail parts to the frame or trucks.

ATS SHOE

Automatic Train Stop, or ATS, is a older type of track signal system in which the signals are received in the locomotive cab, not on some type of trackside indicator. This signal was picked up from the rail by the ATS shoe. This shoe was installed on the front right journal of the front truck.

Not many railroads had this type of signal system, so this particular detail is common only on those roads. Chicago & North Western and Santa Fe were two railroads that protected portions of their trackage with this system.

In model form, the ATS shoe is easy to add. Details West makes a metal casting of the shoe. While they give instructions for installing the shoe, slight modification will produce a more prototypical installation. Remove the center bar with the mounting pin from the shoe. Secure the remaining U-shaped piece to the shell with CA. This is a simple but accurate installation. Another part of the system is a small cylinder-shaped piece that is located along the bottom edge of the frame above the shoe. This part comes with the Precision Scale Co. ATS pick-up shoe. Photo 4-15 shows the ATS shoe and frame piece mounted on a CNW SD45.

This HO scale Missouri Pacific GP15-1 is a virtual scale replica of the real locomotive.

5 Bodies

Now we get to the heart of locomotive detailing. All the details and upgrading in the world on the chassis, underframe, and trucks are a waste of time unless the body is of similar quality and accuracy. As I noted earlier, HO scale model railroaders are indeed fortunate, as the newest releases set higher standards for detail and accuracy. But what if you need an entire fleet of locomotives, some of which have been on the market for years? There are literally dozens of older releases that, while state-of-the-art for their day, no longer measure up to these new units, and there is little hope that manufacturers will upgrade many of these model locomotives. Fortunately, there are hundreds of detail parts that can help you upgrade below-par models and kitbash unavailable models that will approach or equal the newer models in quality.

THE LOWER BODY

Couplers. If you want to get into serious operation or just seek ease of operation, you should install Kadee couplers, or couplers of a similar type. There is no substitute for their appearance or operation. Put those "hook horn" couplers that come with each model in the trash as soon as possible. For those just starting in the hobby, it is best to learn how to install Kadees right away. While the overall fleet cost is the same, it doesn't seem as bad to spend a buck or two per unit as you purchase cars and locomotives rather than to try to upgrade an entire fleet of cars and locomotives later.

The subject of couplers can lead to a great amount of debate. For many years the Kadee coupler has been the industry standard. Their extensive line of coupler shank types and mounting box styles gives you a variety of options. Kadee includes excellent instructions with their couplers. A comprehensive list of coupler conversions and applications are listed in the Walthers catalog. The recent introduction of the similar, operationally compatible Intermountain and McHenry couplers gives

you a lower-cost option. The only drawback to these new couplers is that they are limited to a single style.

Choose a coupler style to suit the application. To add a snowplow to the front of a unit, you will need a coupler with a longer shank so the uncoupling trip pin of another unit does not interfere with the snowplow. For such an application, a Kadee no. 26 coupler in a standard mounting box will work just fine. Other detail or operational requirements will dictate the style and mounting needed.

Regardless of the coupler type you chose for a particular application, the most important part of coupler installation is that the coupler knuckle and trip pin be the correct height. Kadee makes a coupler height gauge that lets you accurately adjust the knuckle, trip pin, and permanent uncoupling magnet to the perfect height.

There are two methods of mounting couplers—body mount and chassis mount. Couplers mounted on the trucks immediately brand the model as a toy train type of unit. If you must use a unit such as this, the coupler mounting should be changed to body or chassis mount for the sake of both operation and appearance.

Manufacturers offer either body or chassis mounts on ready-to-run locomotives. Both accomplish the same purpose by providing a solid, stable platform to mount the couplers. Kato and Atlas locomotives feature both types on their locomotives. The particular type is dependent upon the specific model. In either case, upgrading to Kadee couplers is easy, as the Kato and Atlas pilot openings will accept the Kadee box with the side mounting "ears" removed.

When it's time to do maintenance and repair work, you don't have to remove couplers from units with body-mounted couplers to remove the body from the chassis. However, you must remove couplers from units that have chassis-mounted couplers to take off the body. On one of my Kato SD40s I sawed the coupler mounting pads off the chassis and epoxied them to the appropriate location behind the pilots. This way, you can leave the couplers in place when you remove the body. While it's not a big deal, the fewer times you must remove the couplers, the less potential there is for damage.

Athearn's extensive line of locomotives all have chassis-mounted couplers. The new C44-9W has a cast-on coupler box with a screw-on cover that allows drop-in installation of Kadee couplers. All the other older units unfortunately do not offer this feature. There is a coupler mounting pad cast onto the ends of the locomotive frame onto which a plastic clip holds the Athearn-supplied hook-horn coupler in place. You will need to modify this mounting pad to mount Kadee couplers. Fortunately, Kadee makes an extensive line of couplers with a variety of shanks that make installation relatively easy. The only requirement is that you must drill and tap the mounted coupler for a 2-56 mounting screw. This is quite easy, and once you assemble and install the couplers you'll have

5-1. Make the coupler mounting pad on an Athearn GP40-2 body from five pieces of evergreen .040 ¼" tiles stacked up and secure them with liquid cement. Drill the pad with a no. 50 bit and tap it for a 2-56 screw. Remove the "ears" from the Kadee coupler box so it fits through the pilot opening.

a very satisfactory coupler mounting.

Another unfortunate aspect of the older Athearn coupler mounting is the slot in the lower pilot that lets you remove the body from the chassis without removing the couplers. For easy disassembly, you could leave these large slots as they are, but for the sake of appearance you should fill them in. You will have to remove the couplers from the chassis mounts to remove the body. An easy solution to this problem is to body-mount the couplers.

It's easy to body-mount couplers on Athearn bodies. For my fleet of Athearn diesels, I used Evergreen .040 ¼" tiles for raw material. Use five tiles on each end of the body. Break them off the sheet into their ¼" squares. Stack the tiles inside the pilot. As you add each tile, secure it with liquid cement (fig. 1). The five tiles will bring the coupler mounting surface down to the proper level when using Kadee no. 5 or any other standard shank coupler (photo 5-1). Assemble the coupler

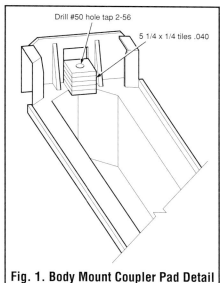

Fig. 1. Body Mount Coupler Pad Detail

mounting boxes with the appropriate couplers and trim the side mount "ears" off the sides of the boxes. Place the assembled couplers on the bottom of the new mounting so the front lip of the mounting box is even with the bottom edge of the buffer plate. Mark the location of the center mounting hole. Drill a no. 50 hole in the mounting pad and run a 2-56 tap into the hole. When you have finished tapping the hole, screw the couplers into place with ³⁄₁₆", 2-56 round-head screws. Snap the body onto the shell, set the locomotive on rails, and use a Kadee coupler height gauge to check the coupler height. In most cases, five tiles will be just about perfect. If the coupler is too high, remove the coupler and cement some thin styrene sheet to the mounting, clear the screw hole, and try again. If the coupler is too low, file some material from the mounting until the coupler height is perfect.

Coupler type is a matter of preference. I use Kadee's no. 5 for the rear couplers and also on the front of units where no snowplow is installed. On snowplow-equipped units, install a long shanked no. 26 in a standard mounting box. Choose the type of coupler you need.

Anti-climbers. Anti-climbers are located on the top edge of the pilots.

5-2. Prepare the front of an Athearn SD40-2 for a larger anti-climber and a pilot-mounted snowplow. File the small anti-climber and the lower pilot detail so they are flush with the pilot face.

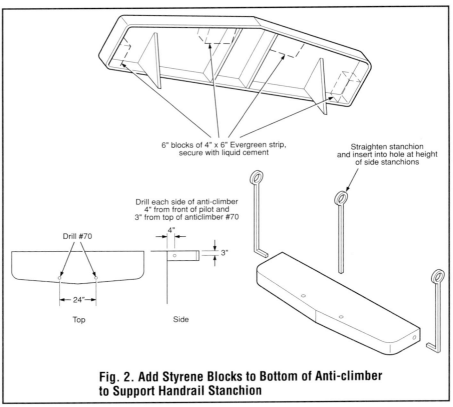

6" blocks of 4" x 6" Evergreen strip, secure with liquid cement

Straighten stanchion and insert into hole at height of side stanchions

Drill each side of anti-climber 4" from front of pilot and 3" from top of anticlimber #70

Drill #70

4"

3"

24"

Top

Side

Fig. 2. Add Styrene Blocks to Bottom of Anti-climber to Support Handrail Stanchion

5-3. Add the new anti-climber, pilot buffer plate, and coupler cut lever.

Some older units have none, some units have a small lip, and others have a large, heavy anti-climber extending from the front and sometimes from the rear as well. Model locomotives generally come with what was standard for the prototype. The Athearn GP38-2, 40-2, and SD40-2 come with the small lip and the GP50 and SD40T-2 come with the large lip or anti-climber.

A popular option on the front of the SD40-2 was the large anti-climber. Details West makes the proper part for this application. Remove the cast-on front lip with a no. 17 blade (photo 5-2) until it is flush with the pilot face, and install the new part with the support brackets (photo 5-3). Before installing the new anti-climber you need to think about handrail stanchion mounting. Figure 2 shows where to install styrene blocks so you can mount the ends of the Athearn stanchions securely.

Sometimes the proper part is already on the locomotive but it is not accurate. Such is the case with the Athearn SD40T-2. Both ends have the large anti-climbers but they are too thin. Rather than replace them, cement a piece of .020 styrene to the bottom of each and trim it to the existing anti-climber contour.

In some cases there are no matching parts available. This is the case with the CN GP40-2LW. The anti-climber is squared off, not angled like the Details West part. On top of that it has a rather complicated edge. Make the new part from a sandwich of three pieces of styrene sheet (fig. 3), using two slightly larger pieces of .015 sheet and a slightly smaller .040 center section. Cement the three pieces together and install them on the GP40 pilot, after you remove the cast-on lip. Use two styrene support brackets to complete the installation. Photo 5-6 shows the completed pilot area.

Buffer plates. Buffer plates are the extended pocket around the coupler itself. Kato, Atlas, the new Athearn C44-9W, and some other units have excellent buffer plates cast on the pilots. The older Athearn units, including the SD40-2, have no buffer plate detail, while the GP38-40-50-60 series have a little top plate detail.

Adding or modifying buffer plate detail on Athearn units is not difficult. Details West makes a metal casting that fits the Athearn SD40-2 coupler opening. With a little filing and fitting the parts fit right in. You can also do this to fill in the lower portion of the pilot. Open the coupler opening on the Details West part to provide clearance for the Kadee coupler box. Photo 5-3 shows the buffer plate installed on a Conrail

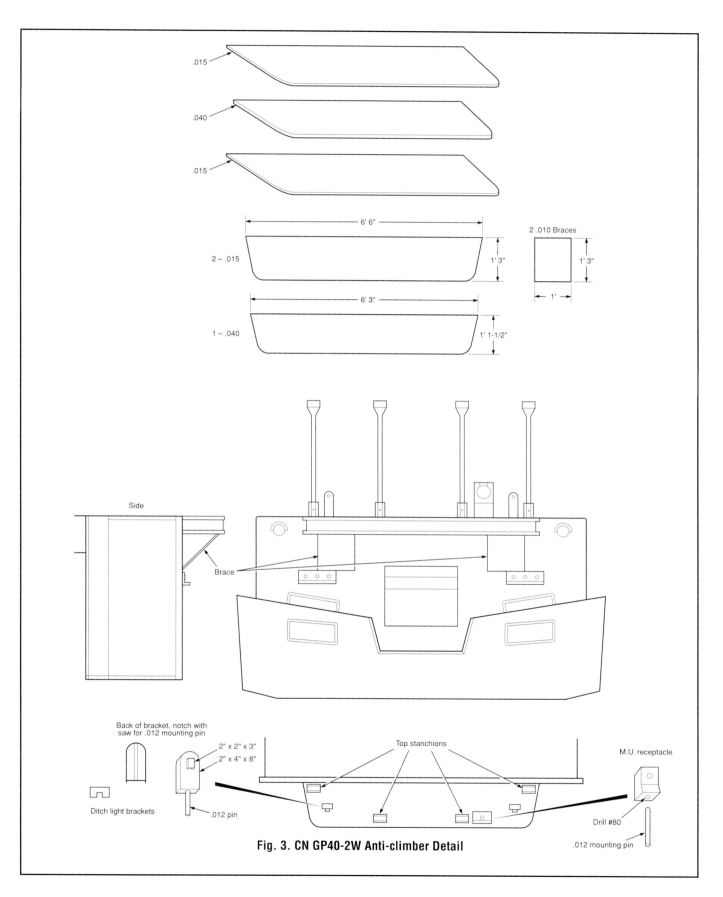

Fig. 3. CN GP40-2W Anti-climber Detail

.015

.040

.015

6' 6"

1' 3"

2 – .015

2 .010 Braces

1' 3"

1'

6' 3"

1' 1-1/2"

1 – .040

Side

Brace

Back of bracket, notch with
saw for .012 mounting pin

2" x 2" x 3"

2" x 4" x 8"

Top stanchions

M.U. receptacle

Ditch light brackets

.012 pin

Drill #80

.012 mounting pin

5-4. As delivered, the center section of the pilot below the coupler pocket is open on the rear pilot of an Athearn GP40-2. First close this area with a piece of styrene sheet that extends right up to the bottom of the coupler box, which has been removed for clarity. The center section of the pilot beam was salvaged from the front of the unit because of a snowplow installation. Trim this salvaged section to fit the opening and secure it with liquid cement.

5-5. You can add more detail to some detail parts, like this Details West metal snowplow. First remove the casting flash from the plow to improve its appearance. Then install grab irons on top of the plow. You can make these grabs from .012 brass wire or modify them from preformed drop grabs. Drill mounting holes in the top of the plow and mount the grabs with cyanoacrylate adhesive.

SD40-2. You can adapt this to fit any of the other Athearn units as well.

Building a buffer plate for the Athearn units from scratch is easy, as it merely surrounds the coupler box. First, fill the lower pilot opening with a piece of .020 styrene sheet. With the coupler in place, fit the new piece right up under the coupler box. It should also be flush with the lower edge of the pilot and flush with the existing pilot face. Use liquid cement to secure it. Reinforce the joints on the back side of the pilot with scraps of styrene. When the cement has set build up the buffer plate with pieces of Evergreen strips. Use a prototype photo as a guide.

There is usually some type of lower pilot detail. In some cases it is just a thin lip on along the bottom of the pilot, while on others it may be a larger pilot beam. Before they were outlawed, there were often footboards on the front of the pilots for the brakemen to ride. On Athearn units where the lower pilot has been filled in, duplicate the lower pilot detail found on either side of the opening for the newly filled-in center section. Build up the new detail from styrene strips or parts salvaged from another unit. In the case of the CNW GP40 shown in photo 5-4, the lower pilot lip was salvaged from

the front of the unit when a snowplow was installed. The salvaged piece was trimmed to fit between the existing rear pilot lower lip and secured with liquid cement.

Snowplows. Most locomotives, with the exception of a few from southern railroads, have some type of pilot-mounted snowplow, some even on both ends. Parts manufacturers have quite a variety of plows to match many prototype styles. To fit a unit with snowplows, first remove all lower pilot detail, as it will interfere with the plow installation. Photo 5-3 shows the lower pilot detail removed in preparation for plow installation.

Fill the open area of the open lower pilots with styrene to the bottom of the coupler mounting box to block off the open area below the coupler. If you don't do this, quite a bit of unprototypical light will appear behind the plow.

Most, if not all, aftermarket snowplows are soft cast metal and they usually include decent instructions and sometimes a template to help with installation. Before installing the plow, use your needle files to remove any molding lines and flash from the plow. Sometimes you will need to make modifications, as a plow may not exactly

match what you are trying to model. A common modification is to remove the M.U. opening doors. While the metal is not as easily worked as styrene, you can file it and cut thin cross sections with a sharp knife. A no. 17 blade works well to shave the doors off the face of the plow. Trim the mounting brackets on the back of the plow if needed to match a prototype application more closely. Be careful when doing any heavy work on the soft metal plows so you don't bend or damage them.

There are few details on plows but one seems to be standard on most larger plows. There are a pair of grab irons located on the top of the plow. Some plow castings even have the location denoted with sets of cast-in dimples. You can modify commercial drop grab irons to match the prototype, but it is often easier to just bend new ones from .012 brass wire to match. There are two ways of mounting the grab irons. One is to cement the grabs to the top of the plow with thickened CA. The other is to drill out the mounting holes and mount the grabs in them, taking care to trim the ends flush with the front surface of the plow. Photo 5-5 shows an out-of-the-package plow and one cleaned up and fitted with grab irons.

Frame lifts

5-6. The pilot detail of the CN GP40-2W shows a number of details common only to CN units. The anti-climber has a unique shape. This one is scratchbuilt. The lower part of the coupler cut lever is a stock Detail Associates part. Bend the coupler level extension from .012 wire and instead of attaching it to the cut lever, mount it in holes drilled into the pilot. This makes a stronger assembly.

5-7. Install a set of A-Line etched stainless steel steps on an Athearn SD40-2. Remove the old steps, but leave a short stub on each side as on the bottom step. Cut the steps from the fret with sharp scissors or a knife on a hard surface. Give the front rear of the step the proper bend and secure the steps with CA.

Now use the template, if included, to mark and drill the required holes. With the locomotive on the rails, position the plow in the mounting holes. There should be at least 1/16" clearance between the bottom of the plow and the top of the rails. If your layout has rough or uneven track, the plow can be raised higher. Should the metal plow contact both rails, it will cause a dead short and stop everything. If the plow doesn't sit level or if the height isn't correct, use a round needle file to elongate the holes to properly position the plow. These enlarged holes will not be visible behind the plow when it is permanently mounted.

If a template is not included, set the locomotive on the rails and set the plow on a 1/16" piece of material or to the height of material you have handy. Mark the pilots where the mounting pins contact the pilot and drill the holes. Again adjust the holes if needed. When the plow has been properly positioned remove it and set it aside. You will add it when you add the final details to the model. When that time comes, use CA to secure the plow to the pilot.

Frame lifts. Pilots on many locomotives built in the last 20 years or so have a simple but not often modeled detail. These are, for lack of a better term, frame lifts and are located at the top

corners of the pilots. They are often no more than a round or oblong hole in the pilots. While some railroads specify a certain style, the locomotive manufacturers have their standard lift opening.

When modeling these openings, be sure to refer to your prototype photos to properly locate and shape them. On most EMD units these openings are diagonal, oblong holes cut into the outside corners of the pilot. You can easily duplicate them by drilling two small holes at the proper location and opening them up with needle files. Clean up the holes with sandpaper to remove any "fuzz" along the edges. On GE units these holes are also oblong, but they are cut vertically into the pilot and often have a reinforcement plate along the top of the opening for added strength. Some shells, the Rail Power C30-7 for example, have the reinforcement plate but no lift opening. To duplicate the openings you need to drill and file them to the proper shape.

Some railroads always have to be different. On CN GP40-2LWs the openings are circular, but they have a semicircular reinforcement over the top half. On these, drill out the opening and model the reinforcement using stanchion mounting guides cut from an Athearn GP7 shell. Shave off four of these and trim the "legs" off the

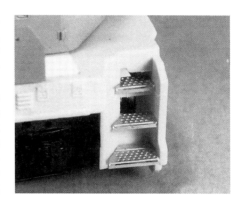

5-8. While A-Line does not make steps for every locomotive, some sets can be used on locomotives for which none are available. Trim a set of steps made for the Rail Power GP35 body to fit the Rail Power SD7 steps. While not a perfect fit, the steps are a tremendous improvement over the cast-on steps.

U-shaped pieces so they form a half circle. Cement these over the tops of the holes. Photo 5-6 shows these lifts on a completed CN unit. On some CP Rail units instead of lift openings, large tabs extend above the pilot. These are available from Detail Associates or can be modeled with .020 styrene and cemented to the corners of the pilots. **Boarding steps.** All units have some sort of boarding steps or ladders. Ladders are relatively easy to deal with. On

5-9. CN GP40-2W locomotives were built with a very different type of step. These steps were more similar to a ladder with a bottom platform. To accurately model these units, you will have to make new steps, as none are commercially available. First remove the old steps as shown. Completely remove all step treads except the bottom one and make a scale 21"-wide opening in each step well.

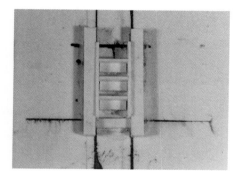

5-10. Construct new steps from Evergreen strips. Using a jig as shown with ladder pieces in place, even if you only build one set of steps.

5-11. Install the completed steps in the opening. Also install an extension of the angled step well, which you can make from Evergreen strip. It should extend to the outside edge of the sidesill.

EMD E and F units they are located on the sides of the units and offer no special challenges to detail. Adding handrails along sides of the ladders and maybe thinning the ladders if they are a little on the heavy side is about all you will need to do to improve these areas. Boarding steps are quite another matter. These are located at the ends right behind the pilots on all road switcher units and even on the full body cowl units like the EMD F45 and the SDP40F passenger units for Amtrak. Some of the newest locomotive releases have beautiful steps. The Proto 2000 SW9/1200 has the most beautiful see-through steps and pilots I've seen. Athearn's new C44-9W also has excellent steps, although they do not have the see-through detail. But what about older models, those with large, sometimes grossly oversized steps? Can they be brought up to these state-of-the-art examples? While on some units it may be very difficult and time-consuming to equal the detail of the best units, there are many ways to improve these areas without spending a lot of money or time.

One low-cost way to improve the step area is to file down the oversized components. Use a flat needle file and remove material from the bottoms of the steps. This is time-consuming, but the result will be thinner and more realistic steps. The steps on some of the early Rail Power shells are examples of such oversized steps and will benefit greatly from the effort.

Another way to improve the step as well as the entire pilot area is to saw off the subpar ends and replace them with ends from a better shell. The ends from an Athearn GP38 or 40 can greatly improve some of the EMD Rail Power shells. While the Athearn steps do not have see-through detail, they are a large improvement. While this is a fairly expensive modification, the cost is reduced further if you use other parts of the Athearn shell for other projects.

A-Line has introduced a relatively recent development in step detail. They are offering an ever-expanding line of etched stainless steel step treads.

Installing these exquisite parts is easy. Saw or cut the old step from the shell, leaving about a 1/16" stub on each side of the step. Cut the new step treads from the etched sheet with sharp scissors, bend according to the instructions, and install with CA. The results are incredible. Photo 5-7 shows an installation sequence on an Athearn SD40-2. While A-Line unfortunately does not have steps available for all locomotives, you can trim some steps slightly to fit other units. With a little trimming, the Rail Power GP35 set will fit the Rail Power SD9 step openings (photo 5-8). Although it is not a perfect fit, it is a vast improvement over the existing steps.

In some cases there is simply nothing available to fit a particular prototype application. Canadian National SD40-2s, GP38-2s, and GP40-2s all have a bottom platform and ladder rather than the standard EMD step arrangement. Modeling this detail is rather involved, but building such a unit with the correct steps will set a model apart from those that are not modified.

When approaching such a conversion, whether it be the CN steps or any other major detail, first determine what if any of the existing part you can use. In the case of the CN steps, retain the bottom step and part of the side ladder support. Remove the middle steps and portions of the side supports (photo 5-9). Build up the new steps with Evergreen strips, using the opening as a guide. In the interest of accuracy and ease of assembly, build a jig (photo 5-10) in which to assemble the parts. While the effort needed to build a jig may not be justified for a single project, if you model the CN and need a fleet of similar locomotives, the time and effort will be well worth it. Locate the built-up ladders in the openings and secure them with liquid cement (photo 5-11). Add an additional strip of styrene to the outside edge of the side ladder support to complete the conversion.

Coupler cut levers. All locomotives have some provision for opening the coupler knuckles. This particular item is called a coupler cut lever or lift bar. There are

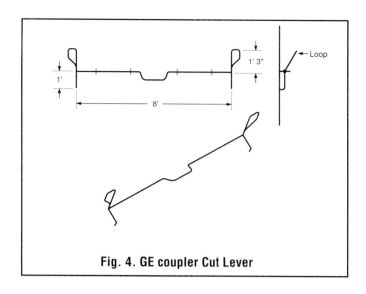

Fig. 4. GE coupler Cut Lever

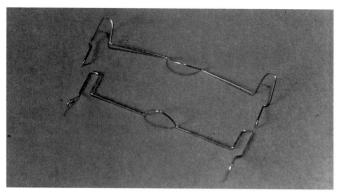

5-12. Some detail parts need a little adjustment before they can be installed. Use the top coupler cut lever straight from the package. However, you will need to "true up" the bends on the bottom part before installation.

quite a few styles, depending on the era and the manufacturer. When modeling early diesel locomotives use a straight-type lever. This simply has the end of the bar bent down to form an "L." On newer locomotives the levers usually have some style of loop or bar extending upward so uncoupling can be performed from the boarding step platform.

Detail Associates has several styles of the cut levers available in sets that will match most EMD applications. There are mounting brackets included in these sets. Installing these levers can be a tedious process. If applying the cut levers on an Athearn unit, remove the cast-on coupler brackets first. A no. 17 blade works well for this. First "true up" the cut levers or have the bends touched up (photo 5-12). Then thread the brackets onto the levers properly and install the ends of the brackets in the mounting holes that were previously drilled in the pilot. Detail Associates has brass brackets that would be an improvement over their plastic brackets. The brass ones are very strong compared to plastic parts. If you're using brass, remove any flash from the bracket and then run a no. 78 bit through the cut lever mounting hole so the lever fits through easily and then install the lever.

GE modelers do not have it as good. The trademark GE "loop" on the extended part of the cut lever is not available commercially in a wire part. Most modelers use the EMD style and ignore the difference. To make a more accurate GE part, use fig. 4 as a guide in bending a lever from .012 brass wire and install as any other cut lever. Photo 5-14 shows such a part installed.

There are a number of variations in the prototype levers. On the CN GP40-2Ws there are unique extensions. These are shown in photo 5-6. Instead of trying to secure the extensions to the cut lever, drill the ends and mount them into the pilot. This is almost impossible to see and is also much stronger.

Ditch lights. Ditch lights are relatively new to the U.S. railroad scene, although our neighbors to the north have had them for many years. There are two basic types of mounting—in-pilot and above-pilot. There are also several styles of light housings. The type of light and location on a particular locomotive are determined by manufacturer or railroad preference. Photo 5-13 shows a set of Detail Associates lights on the Athearn C44-9W mountings.

The in-pilot mounting is the easiest to install. Locate and mount the proper style of light on the front of the pilot. Locate the above-pilot mount on the top of the walkway and secure it with the proper cement. If there is no mounting pin on the bottom of the light housing, make one from small brass wire. The addition of a mounting pin will strengthen the base-to-walkway mounting. Drill a no. 80 hole in the bottom of the mounting bases. CA a short piece of .012 brass wire into each hole. Mark the corresponding pin location on the walkway and drill the same no. 80 hole in each location. Insert the pin in the hole and secure it with liquid cement.

Lighting the ditch lights is an individual decision. Details West includes lights with their ditch lights. You can wire these into the locomotive or add them to a lighting circuit. Some lighting circuit kits include bulbs for the ditch lights. The in-pilot housings are easiest to light because you can drill the hole for the bulb all the way through the pilot, making it invisible. The above-pilot mount will take some ingenuity to light so the wiring will not show.

If you don't opt for lighting, add M.V. Products lenses to improve the look of the lights. Determine the size of the lenses you need and install them with CA in the lens openings.

Drop steps. Drop steps are not a universal detail on locomotives. On locomotives with large anti-climbers, drop steps are not necessary—at least not on the end with the large anti-climber. Some older units without multiple unit capability were also not equipped with drop steps. Some units as recent as a Milwaukee Road GP38-2s built in 1973

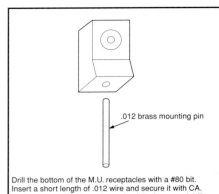

.012 brass mounting pin

Drill the bottom of the M.U. receptacles with a #80 bit. Insert a short length of .012 wire and secure it with CA. Locate the receptacle on the ends of the frame and drill a corresponding #80 hole. Insert the M.U. receptacle and secure it with liquid cement.

Fig. 5. M.U. Receptacle Mounting

5-13. Ditch lights will soon be required on almost all locomotives. There are a variety of styles of both light housings and mounting brackets. Replace the cast-on lights on an Athearn C44-9W with Detail Associates ditch lights.

5-14. Mount the Detail Associates flexible plastic M.U. hoses on the front of a Kato GP35. While these flexible hoses can take some abuse, they can break off. Also, paint and weathering does not stick to them very well, as can be seen by the paint chips.

were not delivered with drop steps, although they were later added.

There are several styles of drop steps, although they are manufacturer-specific styles rather than railroad options. On Atlas, Kato, and Proto 2000 locomotives the proper drop steps are molded in the up position with the end handrail-stanchion castings. The Athearn C44-9W has the rear drop step molded in the down position. Detail Associates offers a good selection of drop steps to fit most applications. Installation instructions are included with the parts, and they can be mounted in either the up or down position. When the steps are mounted in the down position it may be wise to add some reinforcement in the form of a small strip of styrene between the pilot and step. The small area of contact between the step and the pilot makes this a fragile installation. If you wish to "drop" the cast-on steps on the Kato and Atlas locomotives, you might have some problems. On the Kato SD40 the drop steps have a molded-on mounting pin that is integral in securing the center section of the assembly. You can cut the steps from the stanchions and

mount them in the down position. This leaves a hole in the top of the walkway and leaves the inside stanchions loose. Plug the hole with stretched sprue and secure the stanchions with small brass pins drilled through the walkway or leave them loose.

Hoses. There are two types of hoses mounted on the pilots—train line air hoses and M.U. hoses. The train air hoses are located just to the right of the coupler on each end. These can be modeled with Detail Associates Freight Car air hoses. Drill the proper size hole at coupler height just to the right of the buffer plate. Secure the hose with a small drop of CA. Some front hose applications have an extended pipe to clear the snowplow. You can duplicate this by leaving a long end on the hose mounting and bending it to match the prototype. Slightly bend the hose to duplicate the sag of the prototype hose.

M.U. hoses are located on either or both sides of the coupler on units with multiple unit capability. These are generally mounted in groups of three of four on both sides of the coupler. Some older units did not always have a full complement of hoses on both sides.

Refer to prototype photos when dealing with such units.

For modeling purposes there are two types of M.U. hoses—flexible plastic and brass. I have used both types, and they both have advantages and disadvantages. The flexible plastic hoses are cheaper and can be curved to match the prototype sag. But these hoses can break off and the curve "set" in them can slowly straighten. Photo 5-14 shows a C&O GP35 with the flexible hoses. Brass hoses, on the other hand, are slightly oversized and more expensive, but any curve you bend into them is permanent and they are very strong. Photo 5-6 of CN GP40-2W shows a brass hose application. The choice is yours.

Mounting the M.U. hoses can be both very easy and quite difficult. Most model locomotives have the hose locations marked in some manner. Drill the proper size holes following the manufacturer's recommendations and install the hoses. The rear pilot is generally easy. Mount the hoses with CA and give them a prototypical sag. If a snowplow is involved, the front hoses are quite another matter. If the plow is already mounted, it is difficult to thread the hoses through the plow opening and into place. If the plow is loose, secure and thread the hoses through the plow openings when the plow is installed. This works fine for the flexible plastic, but the brass hoses need to be pre-bent. Using either plastic or brass, you will

5-15. This is the pilot of a BN C30-7 with several interesting details. An accurate GE coupler cut lever is not available commercially, so bend one from .012 brass wire. The Detail Associates M.U. hose under the anti-climber is soft metal, so you can position it according to the prototype.

5-16. Walthers has a diesel dress-up kit for F units. The kit includes location templates, a variety of grab irons, clear window, headlight and porthole castings, and complete instructions. In a matter of minutes a modeler can improve even an old shell like the Athearn F7 shown here.

have to make a lot of effort to duplicate the proper sag of the hoses passing through the plow. Nothing looks more unrealistic than these hoses sticking straight out of a plow.

M.U. stands. There are several types of M.U. stands, and the particular styles are generally specific to certain locomotive models. First generation EMD models showed the most variety in the types of stands used. High and low mounts as well as multiple receptacle models were all used. As some of these units were rebuilt the stands were often modified as well. Prototype information is a must to correctly model one of the older units. Early second-generation units all feature low stands of what were called an "intermediate" type, and later units featured the "late" type stands. Again, refer to prototype photos for correct applications.

Detail Associates offers a large complement of the M.U. stands to fit nearly any need. Each set comes with a variety of covers as well. Study your photos to determine the correct cover to use. General information and mounting instructions are included. While the parts are all styrene and can be secured to the walkways with liquid cement, you might

want to strengthen this joint. Make small pins cut from .012 brass wire and secure them with CA into no. 80 holes drilled into the bottom of the M.U. stand. Drill a corresponding hole in the proper location on the walkway and secure the stand with liquid cement. Figure 5 illustrates this procedure.

GE and all current EMD models now have the M.U. receptacles mounted below the top edges of the pilots. If a particular model does not have these molded details or they are inaccurate, you can model them using the Detail Associates M.U. Receptacle set. Drill a small hole in the proper location and cement them in place. A new twist to the M.U. scene is the Details West M.U. cables. Several styles of receptacles are available with cables attached. These are cast in soft metal so the cables can be positioned in a realistic manner. Attach the metal receptacles with CA (photo 5-15). Another detail is unattached cable. You can drape this through stanchions or over a grab iron to represent an unused cable.

NOSE AND CAB

Our attention will now move above the walkway and deal with the

front of the unit. There are many different types of noses and cabs. Each builder has unique plans for these areas. Most designs are strictly a function of the intended use, but in the early years of locomotive production, aesthetics were also considered when designing a locomotive. This resulted in some unique styles.

Perhaps the most famous and popular diesel locomotive nose of all time is the EMD E and F units. In model form there are several examples of these locomotives available. Athearn offers an F7A and B unit which has been on the market for years. The overall detail and accuracy are good but not up to today's standards. Stewart makes an extensive line of F units that ride on a Kato drive. These units feature excellent detail. Highliners offers an F unit with a variety of detail parts; unfortunately, they are only available in B unit versions. Life-Like Proto 2000 offers an excellent, nearly flawless E8-9.

In dealing with the nose and cab of these units there is really not much that can be done other than adding small details if they are not already on the unit. Primary details include window glazing, grab irons, headlights, and

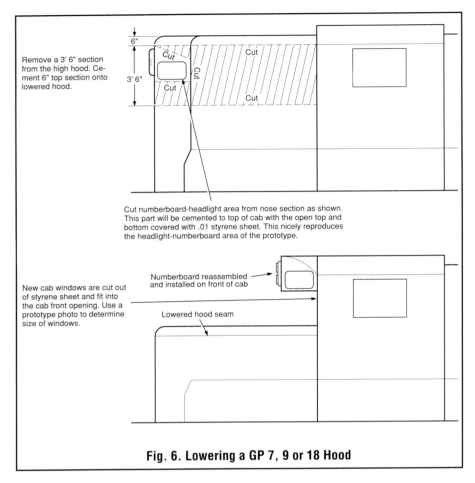

Remove a 3' 6" section from the high hood. Cement 6" top section onto lowered hood.

Cut numberboard-headlight area from nose section as shown. This part will be cemented to top of cab with the open top and bottom covered with .01 styrene sheet. This nicely reproduces the headlight-numberboard area of the prototype.

Numberboard reassembled and installed on front of cab

New cab windows are cut out of styrene sheet and fit into the cab front opening. Use a prototype photo to determine size of windows.

Lowered hood seam

Fig. 6. Lowering a GP 7, 9 or 18 Hood

windshield wipers. Walthers Diesel Dress-up kit includes many of the parts needed to detail the Athearn F unit. The grab irons can be used on any E or F unit. Grab irons can also be bent from brass wire to match the prototype parts. Photo 5-16 shows an Athearn unit with a dress-up kit installed.

By far the most popular type of locomotive by sheer numbers is the road-switcher configuration. This design features a narrow, long and short hood and a standard-width cab with the walkway surrounded by handrails. The basic road-switcher layout is standard among all builders. On this basic design individual manufacturers used their own "standard" components.

The front of the road-switcher design features a short hood. In the interest of crew safety, some railroads denoted the long hood end as the front. For our purposes we will denote the short hood end as the front. As mentioned before, each builder has his own design. There are low and high versions of the short hood.

High noses. The first road-switcher designs featured high short hoods. As railroads recognized the benefits of the increased visibility of a low short hood, manufacturers built units with the low hoods and some railroads "chopped" the high hoods to a lower configuration. The only railroads to choose the high hood design in later models were those that operated long hood forward or had a special operating need for a high hood.

Modeling high hoods on early EMD GPs is easy, as these models come with a high hood. The only exception is the Walthers GP9, which represents a rebuilt or chop-nose locomotive. There are few variations of the early high-hood design. Any additional modeling

work on these hoods is primarily adding details. The usual high short-hood details include grab irons, lift rings, number boards, a sand filler hatch, and a headlight. Some passenger units had their steam-generating equipment located in the high hood. The headlight and sand filler hatch are normally cast on. You must remove and replace these parts to make any detail changes or improvement. Some grab irons and lift rings are also cast on. You will also need to remove these parts to replace them with more accurate wire parts. This is accomplished with a no. 17 X-acto blade. If possible, try to leave the bolt castings on the grab irons. Drill the holes for adding the new grabs in that location.

Later high-hood designs are more difficult to model, as all models of the later designs feature low hoods, with the exception of the old Atlas GP38. Fortunately several parts companies offer high-hood conversions. The Cannon & Co. EMD high hood is suitable for all models from the SD35 on. This exceptional kit features a number of different brake designs to match prototype applications. Detail Associates offers several kits—one for a high-nose Alco "hammer head" conversion and one for a GE high hood.

Adding a high nose to a model is not difficult. The kits include removal instructions. In the case of the GE and EMD high hoods you must cut the old short hood from the rest of the body. You must also remove the number board headlight assembly on the cab until flush with the front of the cab. You don't need to use a Cannon cab with the EMD hood. Assemble and position the new hood where the old hood was removed. Add grab irons, number boards, and roof details according to prototype information.

Low noses. Each manufacturer has its own particular low-hood design. Early EMD units from the GP30 introduced in 1963 through 1977 had a standard 81" long nose. Those from 1977 to the present have a standard 88" nose. To add more confusion, some units that were equipped with remote control radio gear had "snoots" either 116" or 123" long. GE and Alco short hoods for the most parts remained the same with none of EMD's variations.

For the EMD modeler, Cannon & Co. offers a complete line of low hoods. All you need to do is remove the old nose and match a specific prototype nose with the appropriate Cannon part. These noses are incredibly detailed and build up to exact copies of the prototype.

Chopped noses. A frequent modification of older high-nose EMD locomotives involves cutting down the high hood for better visibility. This "chop nose" was done to many GP and SD7s and 9s. Most railroads followed a fairly standard design in lowering the nose, and the previously mentioned Walthers GP9 follows this example. Do not confuse these chopped noses with EMD's low noses, first introduced on the GP9. The factory-built low nose had a noticeable slope from back to front, which the modified units do not copy. Backdating a low-nose Proto 2000 GP18 to represent a chop-nose GP9 will not be accurate. If you are in need of any other chop-nose unit besides a GP9, the best route to take would be to cut the entire nose, cab, and sub-base area from a Walthers GP9 shell and replace the entire area on the new shell. This method would work well on the Proto 2000 and Rail Power SD7-9 shells. Lacking the Walthers shell, you can cut down the high nose just like the prototype. Figure 6 illustrates the sequence. Cut off the top of the high hood, remove a section of the hood, and cement the top section to the lowered nose. The front section of the high hood containing the headlight and number boards is shaped as shown. Add thin styrene to the top and bottom and cement the assembly to the front of the cab. Fabricate the new windshield area from sheet styrene and install it.

As with all locomotive modifications, there is always more than one way of doing things. Railroads such as Illinois Central Gulf and Milwaukee Road, as well as outside contractors have rebuilt locomotives. It is impossi-

5-17. Here is a Cannon & Co. cab, nose, and sub-base assembly. Separate door castings make it easy to build a unit with one or both doors open. In this case the front door is partially open. You should consider adding interior details if you leave a door open.

ble in a book of this size to cover all prototype variations. Using these examples as a guide, you should be able to model nearly any variation by using imagination and ingenuity.

Cabs. The conventional cab of the road switcher is about the same size on most locomotives. The only significant variation is the builder's individual style or design. For modeling purposes we have the model-locomotive-supplied cabs and two Cannon & Co. EMD cabs. For the most part the locomotive-supplied cabs are accurate and well-detailed. Nothing more than detailing need be done to build an excellent model.

There are some cabs that need improvement. The earlier Rail Power cabs are dimensionally correct but poor in detail. EMD modelers are lucky because several options are available. An Athearn cab would improve it greatly. And a beautiful Cannon cab (photo 5-17) would make it even better. GE modelers are not so lucky. About the only replacement option is to find an Atlas cab from their U33C or C30-7. The Athearn GE cab isn't a good fit because the Athearn hood is a scale foot too wide.

The cabs on switchers are no larger that those on road-switchers but

appear so because they lack the short hood or low nose. They also have increased window area to the rear for increased visibility. Aside from any body detail improvements, the single most visible feature is the cab. Cannon offers two types of EMD cabs that cover production from the SW1/NW2 up to the SW1200. With the possible exception of the Kato NW2 and the Proto 2000 SW9/1200, replacing the kit cab with a Cannon beauty will greatly improve any model. To add one of these cabs, remove the old cab and battery boxes down to the frame. Assemble and install the Cannon cab. Because of the large window area, adding a cab interior will definitely be a plus. Keystone Locomotive Works offers an SW cab interior that fills the bill nicely.

The latest type of crew protection is the wide-cab. Although not widely used on road-switchers in the U.S. until recent years, the wide-cab has been in use in Canada since 1973 (photo 5-18). While wide-cab designs are all basically similar, there are quite a few minor variations on the theme. Modeling these cabs is not too difficult, as there are several types available. Detail Associates offers the Canadian cab and three variations of U.S. designs. Model

5-18. This Detail Associates Canadian wide-cab is assembled and ready to install.

5-19. Remove the entire nose section from an Athearn GP40-2 before adding a wide-cab. Remove the electrical filter cabinet and hole fill the hole with sheet styrene. Fill the front of the nose opening with styrene because the wide-cab does not extend as far forward as the cast-on nose did.

locomotive manufacturers have responded to this movement and have introduced several new locomotives featuring wide-cabs in several varieties.

When replacing a conventional cab with a wide-cab, remove the old cab, short hood, and cab sub-base down to the frame. With this done assemble the new cab and test-fit it to the frame. Most of the work in adding the new cab will likely be closing up the remaining gaps on the walkway and the area where the electrical filter box on EMD units was removed. Do this with sheet styrene (photo 5-19). When you have filled all the gaps, cement the cab in place. On some installations you might need some reinforcement on the thin side sill and cab joint. Do this with thin strips of styrene and cement them over the joints.

Sub-bases. Below all road-switcher cabs are the sub-bases. These are often referred to as battery boxes, but the official EMD term for them are sub-bases. Again, the locomotive-supplied parts are quite accurate and detailed but there are prototype options and modifications. GE sub-bases are built more into the frame of the unit and there aren't many options and detail variations. EMD, however, has a number of options and variations. Luckily, Cannon & Co. has again come to the

rescue with a wide variety of these bases that cover the EMDs from the GP30 to the present. Almost any prototype door variation is available in this line of parts. It is a matter of identifying the proper door and installing it.

Before leaving road switchers, I need to say a few words about Cannon & Co. parts. As I mentioned in the previous paragraphs, Cannon makes an extensive line of parts for EMDs. Each area, nose, cab, and sub-base, has a number of parts available to match nearly all prototype second-generation variations. While these parts can certainly be used separately, they really shine when used together. The Cannon cabs, noses, and sub-bases are all designed to fit together perfectly. While not everyone can appreciate the detail of these parts, even the most discriminating modeler cannot find fault with them. For about $20 you can assemble an exquisite nose-cab-base assembly that is without equal. Adding one of these properly detailed assemblies will improve any model.

Cab details. We have dealt with the major cab variations. Now we will address the individual details that are integral to the cab and crew for comfort and operation, and also details that are coincidentally mounted on the cab for the sake of convenience or visibility.

Windows. The most noticeable detail in the cab area are the cab windows and associated hardware. On most prototype locomotives the nonmovable cab glazing is flush with the outside surface of the cab. Kato, Atlas, and Proto 2000 locomotives have decent "glass" and are very passable—the windows are inset from inside, giving the look of nearly flush glazing. All Athearn locomotives except the new C44-9CW lack this detail because the surface of the plastic glazing is flush with the inside surface of the cab. While this may seem like a minor detail, it is surprising how good these units look with flush glazing.

The modeler has two options to improve the windows of the existing Athearn cabs. American Model Builders and Run 8 Productions offer a line of flush-fitting windows that will fit many Athearn and even Rail Power shells. Run 8 windows are vacuum-formed acetate and are noticeably better (photo 5-20), though they have slightly rounded edges. My method of installing these windows differs from the manufacturer's in that I cut all windows apart and install them individually. I don't use the side windows because the plane of these windows extends beyond the framework. Super Jet CA works well to secure these windows from the inside of the cab. The

5-20. Add a few simple details to the front of the cab of this factory-painted Athearn SD40-2, such as flush-fitting Run 8 windows, A-Line windshield wipers, a new horn, and simply painting and decaling the number boards. This makes a tremendous improvement in the looks of this unit.

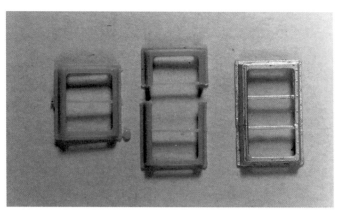

5-21. Some parts are not available. A large, three-frame, all-weather window is one of them. Luckily, you can make this part from available detail parts. The top part is a Detail Associates all-weather window. Combine two of these to make the larger window. The middle parts are the modified pieces. The lower part is a finished enlarged window.

American Model Builders windows are laser-cut to exact tolerances and fit very nicely into the openings. Install these windows from the outside of the locomotive and secure them with liquid cement. When applying the liquid cement, be careful not to mar the windows. A nice feature is a preapplied masking on all windows so you can apply them before painting. After you finish painting and weathering, you can remove the masking.

By far the best windows are found on Cannon & Co. cabs. The Cannon cab parts are cast thin and the back of the window openings are further inset, so that when you install the proper-sized pieces of clear styrene from the back after the model is complete, the windows appear to be flush and the clear surface is right to the edge of the simulated window gaskets. Also model the side windows as separate frames into which you add the glazing. You can position these individual frames in any manner from closed to fully open. While you need to use quite a bit of care when adding the glaze to these window openings, the resulting windows are simply awesome.

Some locomotives have what is called an all-weather window. This is basically an extended side window and is a common feature on some northern railroad locomotives. It is usually installed only on the engineer's, or right, side of the cab because they are quite expensive. Detail Associates offers a double-type window. While this is common for many application, as always some railroads chose a different path. There are some triple-window types. This is quite easy to duplicate using two Detail Associates all-weather windows. Cut just the end from one window and cut through the middle of the other, leaving the center post intact. Cement the two parts together and fill any seam. Photo 5-21 shows this sequence. Paint and glaze this window but don't install it until the unit is complete. Glazing this window is easy before the part is installed. Cut a piece of .005 clear styrene to fit inside the window, making sure the glazing extends all the way to the edges of the frame, and secure it with liquid cement. Glaze the narrow end window with a Micro-Scale product called Kristal Kleer, which looks like white Elmer's Glue but dries clear. Work it around the edge of the window openings to form a liquid "cover" and let it dry.

Railroads made some early all-weather windows from wood framing, plywood, and glass. The Minneapolis & St. Louis Railroad was one such road. You will need to scratch-build this project using a photo of the unit as a guide.

Some locomotive cabs have additional side windows. This was standard equipment on many early GE units. Soo Line even ordered a number of SD40 and SD40-2s with additional side windows. Athearn and some Atlas GE cabs have these extra side windows. Detail Associates offer these extra windows for EMD units. When the Federal Railroad Administration mandated that all windows be high-impact safety glazing, almost all of these extra windows were plated over rather than given the additional expensive glazing. Plating the model windows is easily accomplished with .005 styrene sheet. Cut the plates slightly larger than the opening and slightly round the corners (photo 5-22). Fill the windows on Athearn U-boats with Detail Associates GE window plugs.

Sunshades. The side locomotive windows usually have some type of adjustable sunshade. Detail Associates offers both plastic and brass shades and A-Line offers a brass shade. The plastic shades look good but break off easily. Mount the A-Line brass sunshade with two thin brass tabs and insert them into holes you have drilled in the sunshade

Rear-view mirror

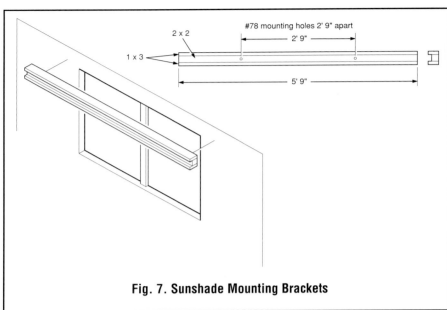

Fig. 7. Sunshade Mounting Brackets

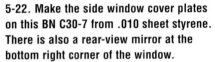

5-22. Make the side window cover plates on this BN C30-7 from .010 sheet styrene. There is also a rear-view mirror at the bottom right corner of the window.

tracks. The brass mounting tabs let you adjust the shade. Some model cabs lack the mounting track. You can get these from the Cannon cab kits, which is an expensive option, or you can make them from Evergreen strips, although they will be slightly oversized. Figure 7 illustrates this sequence. Some locomotives have shades shaped slightly differently. You can modify the A-Line brass shades or you can cut them from .010 styrene sheet and install them.

Cab deflectors–mirrors. Many locomotives have cab deflectors mounted on each side of the cab side windows. Detail Associates offers several styles of these parts. Some types of deflectors also serve as rear-view mirrors. Refer to prototype information when choosing deflectors for a certain locomotive. When not in use these deflectors are normally flat against the side of the cab; when in use they are positioned away from the cab. When adding plastic deflectors to a locomotive it is best to use CA and cement them to the side of the cab rather than try to position them away, as they will break off easily

(photo 5-23). Detail Associates also offers a set of etched-brass deflectors that you mount with wire eyebolts. While this arrangement offers some flexibility in positioning, the oversized eyebolts will detract from the overall appearance of the unit.

Some railroads install rear-view mirrors similar to car mirrors on the sides of some locomotives. BN and Santa Fe have commonly done this. There may be commercial examples of these small mirrors, but you can make them easily from a small piece of wire and a bit of thin styrene strip using the particular prototype mirror as an example. Photo 5-22 shows a small mirror installed on a BN C30-7.

Armrests. Armrests are another common detail. These are located right below the side windows. Some locomotive cabs already have these details cast on. If you don't need them, slice them off. If they are not on the cab and should be, Detail Associates offers two styles. Locate them using prototype information.

Windshield wipers. One detail that is common to all locomotives is the windshield wipers. Several manufacturers offer these parts, but I use A-Line wipers exclusively. These are exquisite parts that will fit most applications.

Drill a no. 78 mounting hole in the proper location and install the proper wiper blade with a small drop of CA on the end. Another reason to have flush windows is that deep-set windows will leave the wipers dangling in thin air, while flush windows will let the blades rest on the surface of the window. Photo 5-20 shows A-Line wipers installed on an Athearn unit.

Headlights. A variety of lights are located around the cab and nose area of the locomotive. The most prominent is the headlight. Depending on the locomotive design and railroad preference, you can mount headlights on either the locomotive nose or above the windshield between the number boards. Most modern locomotives now use only a single set of headlights. This was not always the case, as early diesels often had several sets of headlights, one regular and often one oscillating Mars- or Pyle-type headlight. SP outdid its competitors with two sets of headlights and a red warning light mounted at the top of the group (photo 5-24).

There are many headlight castings available. Most modern diesels mount what detail manufacturers term the "Dual Pyle Late Type." On most conventional cab EMD units, mount them vertically on the front of the unit

5-23. Cement the wind deflectors, by Detail Associates, to the side of the cab to prevent them from breaking off. Secure clear parts with CA, which does not attack the plastic like liquid cement.

5-24. Mount the headlights on the SPGP9 nose and cab. Mount a Pyle Gyralite above the nose headlight. While the unit is rebuilt, move the Gyralite to the roof of the cab. After painting, install the Gyralite above the cab-mounted headlight.

and horizontally on the rear. When mounted over the windshield on the front they usually have a small shield to keep stray light off the locomotive nose. It is important to work from prototype photos to choose the proper style lights and locate them properly. Some roads did specify a short hood mount, in which case plate over the upper mounting location. Cannon cabs have this detail. Santa Fe originally ordered the high-mount lights but has since relocated the front headlights to the low nose.

Changing headlights can range from easy to quite difficult. A simple headlight change may involve nothing more than slicing off the old part and adding the new one. Nose-mounting a headlight can range in difficulty from just filing a flat spot on the nose, as on CP Rail units, to notching the nose to install a Details West "Pyle Twin Gyralight Flush Mount," as used on some DRG&W units. These come with installation instructions. In most cases, open up the nose only enough so the detail part fits properly in the opening. Careful work here will result in a tight fit and will prevent gaps that would be difficult to fill.

Classification lights. Classification lights are another detail. These lights

are no longer required, so new units are no longer delivered with them, and many railroads are in the process of removing these lights as locomotives are shopped. The railroads may paint over the blanked-out lights, bolt a blank cover over the opening, weld sheet steel over the openings, or fill the openings so that no traces of the their former location remain.

Those detailing earlier models will find both the class lights and their location to be fairly standard. Both EMD and GE mounted these lights high on the low nose and near the middle of the rear nose. Of course there are always variations. For some of their later units Conrail chose a "bug eye" type of light. This type of class light is available in the Cannon & Co. cab kits. Some Canadian units have a three-light class light system that you must scratchbuild. Again, refer to prototype information when dealing with these details.

Step lights. Step and ground lights are located at several points around prototype locomotives with location depending on railroad preference. The most consistent application is at the bottom of the locomotive frame below the cab right behind the front jacking pads. The engineer uses these lights in dark areas to see if the train is indeed

moving and not slipping when starting out. Mount the Details West step light in the proper-sized hole in this location. Some frames are too thin to be drilled, so cement a small piece of styrene to the inside of the frame as a backer and then drill it. Install these with CA. The Southern Railroad mounted these lights along the top of the long hood as walkway lighting. Refer to prototype photos to place these lights accurately.

Number boards. Number boards are carried on all locomotives. These items are located at each end of the locomotive and are usually lighted for nighttime identification. Model manufacturers have generally done a good job in dealing with these details. Some number boards, like the Athearn SD40-2 rear number boards, are just a lip cast onto the locomotive surface, while others are clear plastic inserts suitable for lighting.

There are only a few cases where the number boards need modification. Some BN C30-7s are just such a case. The rear number boards on the Rail Power C30-7 shell represent an early version applied to this locomotive. Some of BN's units are later production C30-7s and have flush-mounted rear number boards rather than the raised versions. To build an accurate version of

5-25. The rear of what will become a BN C30-7 shows a number of modifications and detail improvements over the original Rail Power shell.

this locomotive, remove the rear number boards until flush with the surrounding rear nose. To make it totally accurate a thin gasket should surround the number boards. This would be very difficult to reproduce in model form, so cut new number boards from .010 styrene sheet and cement them to the rear nose (photo 5-25).

Lighting and warning beacons. Illuminating the various locomotive lights is a matter of personal preference. The Kato, Atlas, and Proto 2000 locomotives come with a decent lighting system. Athearn units, on the other hand, come with a bare bulb that lights up the entire front of the unit; the exception is the new C44-9W, in which the bulb is contained in a small housing and just lights the nose headlight.

While lighting supplied by the manufacturer may be adequate for many, some companies offer lighting packages for a variety of locomotive applications and functions if you want state-of-the-art lighting. All kinds of options are available—constant lighting, directional lighting, flashing warning beacon, and an assortment of accessory lights. You can find these options singly or in combinations from a variety of manufacturers.

To install a lighting system you must choose a lighting package that is compatible with your locomotive, and you must be able to solder the wiring into the locomotive electrical system. The lighting kits usually have excellent instructions to help you easily install a new lighting circuit. Photo 5-27 shows an On Track LTD lighting circuit installed on a Rail Power C30-7 shell.

For a number of years an amber roof beacon was required on all loco-motives. These were usually installed on the cab roof for maximum visibility. There are several types and Details West offers the two most-used varieties. Again, prototype photos are a must to locate these details accurately, especially on older locomotives. Photo 5-26 shows a beacon installation. I sometimes think railroad shop workers purposely vary locations of various items to drive modelers nuts. Since these beacons are no longer required, new locomotives are no longer delivered with them and many railroads have since removed these items.

Beside the amber beacon there are a variety of white strobe lights applied to some locomotives. Amtrak F40PH locomotives have a pair of these at the top front corners of the cab. These are generally smaller than the amber beacons and will likely have to be scratch-built to match prototype applications.

Nose bell. Another nose-mounted detail on some units is a gong-type or round bell. This bell is mounted on some Chicago & Northwestern and Detroit, Toledo and Ironton units. For the simplest installation file a flat spot on the front the nose and install the bell. This does not do justice to the installation. The bell is actually mounted on a housing that is slightly inset into the nose. Figure 8 shows a construction and installation sequence

5-26. To make this a Milwaukee Road GP38-2 you will need to add a variety of detail parts to the cab roof area of this Athearn unit.

5-27. Install a lighting kit on a Rail Power C30-7. These kit are usually quite easy to install and only require several solder connections. Be sure the kit you plan to install will work on your chassis, as some kits are designed for Athearn units and will not work properly on can-motor-equipped units and vice versa.

Cut nose bell openings before assembling the cannon nose.

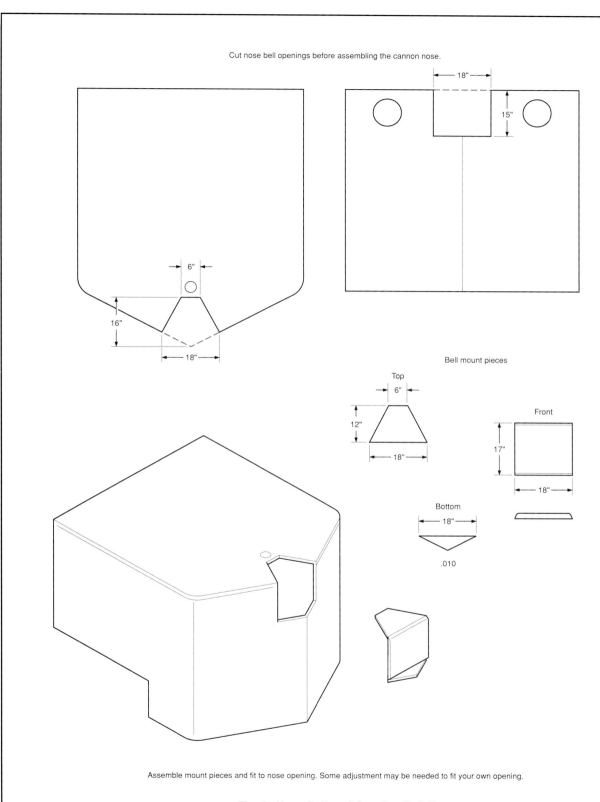

Bell mount pieces

Top

Front

Bottom

.010

Assemble mount pieces and fit to nose opening. Some adjustment may be needed to fit your own opening.

Fig. 8. Nose Bell and Opening Detail

5-28. The front of this heavily modified Rail Power SD45 shows an assortment of detail parts and modifications.

5-29. The rather complex antenna arrangement on the roof of a Southern Pacific SD40-T2 is for remote locomotive control. The antenna platforms are Details West parts, the antenna conduit is .012 brass wire running through Detail Associates wire eyebolts, the antenna on the large platform is a DA whip antenna, and the antennas on the small platforms are small nut-bolt-washer castings.

that looks prototypical on a model. Photo 5-28 shows an application of this detail on a CNW SD45; the bell will be installed after painting.

Horns. Horns are one of those items that can be found almost anywhere on the roof of a locomotive, although they are normally somewhere around the cab. For many years, from the GP35 through the SD60, the standard EMD horn location was on top of the number board–headlight housing unless moved or otherwise specified by the individual railroad. GE units had a little more variety with some horns located on the cab and many mounted on the long hood behind the cab. The current trend is away from the cab to reduce noise in the cab.

Horns come in a wide array of styles and for modeling purposes. You only need to match the look and location of the horn. Without going into the mechanics of horn sound you must determine what type of horn is used on your prototype. Again there is some standardization on many EMD units, like the Details West "Leslie RSL-3L-R" horn that matches most applications almost exactly. This horn is installed on the Milwaukee GP38-2 shown in photo

5-26. Other applications may require some detective work. Several trains use three- and five-chime horns. Details West has a variety of cast-brass horns in addition to the previously mentioned Leslie horn. Detail Associates has a variety of plastic horn kits in which the frame, diaphragm, and chime are separate parts and can be assembled to match a specific horn. These kits are great, but the completed horns are quite delicate and will not tolerate much abuse. Brass horns are much stronger and preferable.

Radio antennas. A variety of radio antennas are mounted on or near the cab roof. The most common antennas are used for radio communication and are of several types. The Sinclair, whip, and firecracker are the most used types. Exact prototype mounting varies, but most are located near the center or rear-center of the cab. Some railroads use an antenna platform, which is mounted behind the cab over the internal filter hatch on EMD units. A good overhead photo will reveal the exact location and antenna type.

Newer units also have another smaller type of antenna for reactive telemetry from the End-of-Train

devices. Many of these look like small versions of the Sinclair antennas. These are also offered in model form.

Another type of antenna system involves remote locomotive control. Southern Pacific has a number of locomotives equipped with this system. Photo 5-29 shows a Southern Pacific with this installed.

Air conditioners. A few railroads give some comfort to their engine crews by installing air conditioners. Except on the new Athearn and Kato C44-9 locomotives, air conditioners are a detail that must be added to a locomotive. Several parts manufacturers offer the two main types of air conditioners. These air conditioners on road-switcher units are located on the cab roofs. On all EMD locomotives, the flat roof provides a perfect base for installation. The curved GE U and dash 7 series roof requires you to use an adapter from the Details West Prime air conditioner. Use prototype photos for the proper location and type of air conditioner.

Vents. A variety of vents sprout from the cab and nose of many diesels. Details West and Detail Associates offer both round and rectangular vents. The rectangular vents are used on the sides of some EMD conventional cabs, and their placement varies. The round vents are commonly mounted on the roofs of both EMD and GE cabs in various locations. Another common use for the round vent is on the right side of the EMD short hood as a toilet vent, but again this is not universal. Accurate use and placement depends on good photos.

Sand hatches. Sand hatches should be included on every model. With sand reservoirs located at each end of a locomotive there are at least two hatches on each locomotive. These details are normally included on most models. On EMD units, from the GP35 on and GE units from the U-series on, these parts will be flat unless they are cast as separate details. It's easy to remove these cast-on parts and replace them with Detail Associates sand fillers. Detail Associates and Details West also make a variety of early EMD and GE hatches that can replace subpar cast-on parts.

Hand brakes. There are several styles of hand brakes on locomotives. All GE and some late EMD units use a brake wheel, while most early EMD units use a ratchet hand brake. All conventional cab GE units have the brake wheel mounted on the side of the short hood. Early EMD road switchers had a brake ratchet mounted on the rear nose or inset into the rear right side of the long hood, most notably the SD45s. Some SD40s have a brake wheel mounted on a separate stand at the rear of the unit. Most second generation EMD units have the ratchet style mounted on the left side of the low nose. Post-1990 EMD conventional cabs have a brake wheel. The introduction of the wide-cab on EMD units has again sent the hand brake to the left rear of the long hood.

The Alco RS and RSD series have their brake wheels mounted on the front of the short hood, while the Century series have ratchet types mounted on the left side of the short hood.

Most model-locomotive-supplied hand brakes could use some improvement. The ratchet-type brakes are

usually nothing more than a simple impression of the real thing. On the Kato SD40 the brake ratchet is only inset about 3 scale inches. The most accurate way to improve the ratchet detail is to replace the stock 81" EMD nose with a similar 81" Cannon short hood. If you don't have the time or money to do this, you can do a little detail improvement.

Details West offers both a ratchet and brake wheel that will work well for most applications. The Cannon & Co. short-hood kits also include these detail parts. In the case of the Athearn ratchet, you can remove the cast-on detail with a no. 17 blade. If you're using the Details West ratchet, remove the "chain guide" from the bottom of the ratchet head, cement the ratchet arm on the head, and install the part in the opening.

In the case of the Kato SD40, you should open up this area to give the notch more depth. Disassemble the model and cut out the inset ratchet area completely. Use a piece of styrene sheet to back the new opening and add the ratchet of your choice.

A common modification, although not completely accurate, can be done to the Athearn SD40-2. The Athearn unit represents a later production unit with an 88" nose and a brake wheel. Earlier versions of the SD40-2 have an 81" nose with a ratchet-type brake. You can back-date the Athearn model with a few simple modifications. The most accurate way to do this is to replace the nose with a Cannon 81" nose. However, many modelers may choose to ignore this extra 7" of short hood. You can convert the brake wheel area to a ratchet notch with a little work. Scrape and sand the brake wheel and associated details from the side of the nose. Using a prototype photo as a guide, cut a notch into the side of the nose in the proper location. Back the opening with some sheet styrene and add the ratchet of your choice.

On Athearn, Rail Power, and any other units with a poor or oversized brake wheel, using a Cannon or Details West part will be a great improvement.

5-30. The Bachmann Spectrum F40PH comes with separate wire grab irons already installed. While the wire grabs may be passable, the grab iron mounting holes and bolt castings are much too large to look good close up. Slice off the cast-on bolts with a no. 17 X-acto blade and plug the oversized grab mounting holes with stretched sprue. Trim the ends of the sprue flush and drill holes for new grab irons.

Grab irons. Grab irons are a common detail on all locomotives. Locations of these details vary according to locomotive builder and the need to access areas of the locomotive for servicing.

On many older model locomotives the grab irons are cast onto the surface of the model. While not overly offensive, these cast-on parts just don't cut it today. If you want to improve the looks of a locomotive, then you must replace these details.

A no. 17 blade works well for removing these details. For this operation I use a blade I have modified slightly with a sharpening stone. I remove the sharp corners from the no. 17 blade, leaving only the sharp middle section. This prevents those corners from nicking and gouging the model surface. On some shells you may wish to leave the bolt casting at the ends of the grabs intact. These details are on the prototype, and will save you the work of replacing them if you need them. They also provide an accurate reference point for the replacement grabs. When the

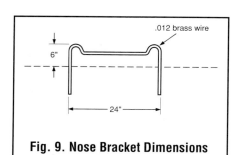

Fig. 9. Nose Bracket Dimensions

5-31. Four brackets are located on the nose of this F40PH. Make these from .012 brass wire and bend it with tweezers. If you plan to make several, make a small jig so the part is uniform.

grabs have been removed, the area can be lightly wet-sanded to remove any traces of the old parts. It is very important to properly space the grabs irons and line up the holes both vertically and horizontally. It is surprising how easily the eye picks up misalignment of these parts. Mark the location of the new grabs carefully with a sharp instrument and drill with a no. 80 bit. It is sometimes best to leave the grab irons off until painting and decaling are complete to avoid problems with masking and decal application.

If you purchase factory-painted units, you might not want to disturb the paint to add such details. On the Athearn SD40-2 where the cast-on grab irons are not grossly oversized, you can apply wire grabs right over the top of the cast-on parts without disturbing the paint. The hole locations are marked

with a sharp instrument and drilled with a no. 80 bit. Install and brush-paint the grabs to match the prototype.

Luckily, some manufacturers have responded to modelers' requests and no longer cast on these details. Athearn adds the bolt castings and molds on small dimples to locate the holes, while Rail Power just uses dimples to mark the grab locations. Do not rely on those cast-on dimples as a drilling guide. The drill bit still may wander off. Mark the holes with a sharp instrument before drilling.

Some of the more recently introduced models now come with separate cast-plastic grab irons that mount into pre-cast holes in the body. While these are a great improvement over the old cast-on grabs, I prefer wire parts. Regardless of improved casting technology I think that a wire part looks better for this application. This modification seems too easy—just substitute wire parts for the cast parts and call it done. Unfortunately, the cast holes in the body are oversized for wire parts. To do the job right you must fill the holes in and re-drill them. You can do this several ways. If the holes are quite small you can use your favorite body filler. Place a small dab on your finger or some type of small spatula and push the filler into the hole from inside the shell until the filler is flush with the top of the hole. Let it dry. Repeat for all holes. I have used this method several times and it works well. Another method is to use thickened CA. Apply a small drop to the back of the hole. Use a small-diameter wire and prod the CA into the hole until it is even with the top of the hole, and let it cure. Using an accelerator to cure the CA will enable you to drill new holes in a matter of minutes. On models where the cast-in holes are quite large, such as on the Bachmann Spectrum F40PH, it may be better if the holes are plugged with styrene rod or, in the case of the F40PH shown in photo 5-30, stretched sprue. Secure the sprue with liquid cement and when dry, trim and sand it smooth.

There are some styles of grab irons or brackets that are not available commercially. The F40PH shown in photo

5-32. Add a new electrical cabinet filter to the rear of the cab on this SD45 model. The realism this adds as a separate part, versus a cast-on detail, is evident in this photo.

5-31 has a number of these items in several locations. Use fig. 9 as a guide in bending these parts from .012 brass wire. Quite a few other styles exist, and they can be reproduced using the same wire to match almost any prototype application.

Cab steps. On EMD conventional cab units there are small step treads located at the two cab door corners of sub-bases. On most EMD models these are cast as solid steps and are quite oversized. If you add a Cannon sub-base kit, you can correct this because the kit includes accurate plastic see-through steps. The A-Line etched boarding step set also includes these steps. If you add this type of set to a unit, you may just as well replace the cab steps. Remove the cast-on steps, leaving only a small stub on each side to support the new etched step. Position and secure them with CA.

Electrical filter cabinets. A detail exclusive to later EMD conventional cab units is the electrical cabinet filter. This detail is located right behind the left side of the cab. This detail first appeared in the late 1960s and continued through the SD60. There are several styles of filter cabinets, and it is always best to check prototype photos

5-33. After installing the Athearn handrails, pinch the top loop of the stanchions firmly with needle-nose pliers and secure the joint further with a small drop of CA.

5-34. The handrails on the MP GP15-1 are offered as a kit by Smokey Valley, which also makes the GP15-1. Mount the front stanchions into the top of the walkway along the edge of the pilot. File the square mounting pins on the stanchions until slightly rounded so they mount easily. Drill the mounting holes no larger than needed, so the stanchions fit tightly. Use CA to secure the stanchions.

to be accurate. Many EMD models come with these parts cast on. While this may be adequate for most modelers, modeling the cabinet as a separate detail will produce a better-looking detail (photo 5-32). The Kato SD40 has this part cast on, though early production SD40s did not have the cabinet, so if need be you'll have to remove the part. To change or remove the cabinet you will have to remove the old cast-on part, fill the hole, and add the new part.

Handrails. Virtually all locomotives with the exception of the early carbody units, EMD E and F units, Alco PA and FA, etc., have handrails. On conventional road-switcher units these handrails surround the locomotive. While the handrails and associated stanchions are quite small and thin, these details are large on our model locomotives, as they are very visible. There is a great amount of debate about the various handrails offered on models. Handrail size, stanchion detail, mounting, and overall accuracy are important considerations. The final decision regarding any replacement, improvement, or modification of these items is yours.

Manufacturers treat handrails differently. Atlas, Kato, Walthers, Bachmann, Stewart, and Proto 2000 all cast the handrail-stanchion assemblies in a flexible plastic that fit into cast-in holes in the frame and cab. This makes these very easy to mount. One major drawback is that the handrails are slightly oversized compared to the prototype, but most modelers can easily live with this problem.

Athearn, on the other hand, has had wire handrails and steel stanchions since they began producing models. These are a little more difficult to apply, as everything comes in pieces to be assembled. The handrails come pre-bent with only some slight bending required for a good fit. Thread the proper stanchions over the handrails and position everything in the mounting holes and secure them with CA. While these handrails are also a little oversized, they are smaller than most cast handrails and when assembled make a strong assembly.

Installing the Athearn handrails is not difficult, but certain steps can make the assembly easier for beginners. First drill out all the stanchion mounting holes with a no. 70 bit and the handrail mounting holes with a no. 76 bit so everything will fit where it is supposed

to—paint sometimes closes up the holes slightly. Now trim off the ends of the handrails that mount into the side of the cab to about $1/16$" so the ends do not interfere with the cab glazing later. Place all the handrails in their proper positions without stanchions. Check all bends and adjust as needed and remove. Before installing the stanchions, check the top loop for correct shape, and make sure that the bottom 90 degree bend is indeed square. When everything checks out, thread the proper number of the correct-length stanchion on each handrail. Doing one set at a time, push the ends of the handrails into their mounting holes and push the bottom of the stanchions into the mounting holes. Check that everything is straight and square. When all the sets have been installed, square up all the stanchions with the handrails and squeeze the top of the loop shut with needle-nose pliers (photo 5-33). Then secure all joints with a small drop of CA. When the CA has set, remove the middle section of the pilot handrails with a rail cutter or a cut-off disk on a Moto-tool.

The extensive line of Rail Power units do not come with any handrails

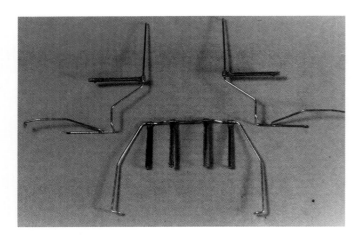

5-35. Here are the front and short hood handrail assemblies for an ATSF SD26. The stanchions are Smokey Valley cast-brass parts. Bend the handrail from .019 brass wire. The same assemblies will fit a SD7 or 9 locomotive.

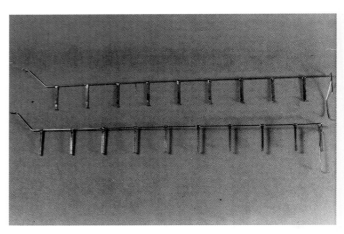

5-36. Make the side handrail assemblies for an ATSF SD26 from Smokey Valley stanchions and .019 brass wire.

or stanchions. You must decide what type to use. Some Rail Power instruction sheets include a handrail bending template so you can bend your own. You can mount these handrails with Athearn stanchions. One option suggested on the SD45 instruction sheet is to use the handrails from an Athearn SD45. Smokey Valley has a number of handrail kits for Rail Power shells and quite a number of other locomotives. These kits are the most accurate option available for any locomotive.

Installing these sets is not much more difficult than installing Athearn handrails. The first step is to clean up the stanchions. Remove any remaining mold residue with a wire brush and any flash with a file. Check the fit of the mounting pin in the mounting hole and clean out the holes if needed. Some pilot stanchions may need to be mounted on the top edge of the walkway. Drill a hole to fit the stanchion mounting pin. The stanchions can now be positioned in their proper locations (photo 5-34). Position the handrails on the unit. If mounting holes are needed, drill them using prototype plans or photos as a placement guide. Adjust any misformed bends, and when everything is properly aligned press the handrails into the stanchion notches.

There are two ways of securing the handrails to the stanchions, with CA or

solder. CA will do a decent job but solder is superior in strength. If you decide to use CA, just touch a small drop to the back of each stanchion-handrail joint and the handrail-to-body joints, and the handrails are complete. If you decide to solder you may be able to solder the joints with everything still mounted on the model. This is extremely risky because any slip will cause serious damage when the hot tip hits styrene. If you are not comfortable with this, remove the entire handrail assembly. If the stanchions-to-handrail joint is quite tight, you may be able to remove each assembly intact and solder it. If the parts do not hang together, you many need to make a template to lay out the pieces or measure each stanchion position before soldering it to the handrail. When the railings are complete it is usually easier to paint the handrails separately and add them later, so do not attach them to the body yet.

While kits are available for many applications, there are times when nothing is available to fit a particular application. Luckily, Smokey Valley and several other manufacturers offer separate stanchion castings for both EMD and GE units. The most difficult part will be bending the new handrails. Actually, it is not that difficult to bend new handrails, and there are several ways of going about this process. One is

to find a scale drawing of the locomotive and use it as a guide in bending the new handrails. If you can't find one, make a scale drawing of the major body features including the attachment points for the handrails. Draw in the new handrails using prototype photos as a guide for locating jogs and bends. Then bend the handrails over this drawing. Push the stanchions into their mounting holes on the model and set the newly bent railing into place. Adjust any bends and when satisfied, secure them to the stanchions.

Another method is to have the stanchions in place and use your eyes to judge the bends. While this is less than accurate, it is surprising how well the eye can judge the prototype bends. While it may take a little practice, this is a relatively fast and accurate way to bend new handrails. The handrails for an ATSF SD26 were bent by eye. Photos 5-35 and 5-36 show the front and side assemblies respectively before they were installed. As to the size of the handrails, prototype handrails are 1¼" in diameter, and Detail Associates .019 brass wire is a perfect match. While paint will add several thousandths of an inch to the diameter, this will be a perfectly acceptable size.

Often when modifying a locomotive you will have to alter or totally replace the handrails. Converting an

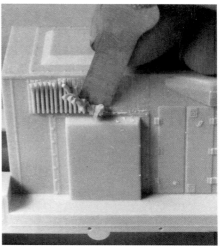

5-37. This CNW C425 started as an Atlas Phase 1 unit. To modify it into an accurate Phase 2 unit you must change the handrails. The cast plastic Atlas handrails can't be modified, so use Athearn stanchions and brass wire to make new handrails. However, you can salvage the inboard stanchion–drop step part of the handrails on the front and rear of the unit. Make the outboard "Y" stanchions by cutting and bending a regular stanchion to match the prototype.

5-38. Remove the internal filter grills by carving away as much material as possible and then scraping and sanding the area smooth.

Atlas model of a "phase 1" Alco C425 to a "phase 2" version requires extensive handrail modifications. Replace all four sets of side railings. For my CNW model I used Athearn stanchions and bent new handrails from brass wire. The front and rear assemblies also needed modification, but instead of replacing everything I managed to salvage the drop step and inside stanchions from the Atlas model. I cut the Atlas handrails flush with the side of the stanchions and drilled holes to accept the .019 brass wire I used for the new handrails. I made new outboard "Y" stanchions from a regular Athearn stanchion and cut and bent part of another to match the prototype. Photo 5-37 shows the front of the C425 modified in this manner.

LONG HOODS

The long hood of a locomotive is the area behind the cab of a unit that houses the engine and most if not all major accessories and components. As modelers we are not concerned with the machinery behind the sheet metal unless we model a unit with hood doors open. We are, however, concerned with the visible portion of those components. The basic mechanical operation of all diesel locomotives are very much the same. The location and appearance of components that support this operation are not. Studying the location of various components on EMD, GE, and Alco road switchers reveals some of these differences.

Hood doors. The sides of the long hoods have a variety of details. On the conventional road switcher the most numerous of these details are the hood doors. Most locomotive models have a unique door arrangement. If you need to do a major kitbash of a unit, the hood doors become a major concern. When kitbashing a locomotive, you might need to piece hood sections together like a jigsaw puzzle to get the proper door arrangement. For EMD units, Cannon & Co. has an extensive line of hood doors. These individual parts can be combined to make a variety of prototype hood door arrangements. In fact, Cannon has such an extensive line of EMD parts including radiator and internal filter screens, internal filter hatches, blower housings, and long hood ends that you could build a complete and accurate EMD long hood for a variety of models if

you built the basic body from styrene (with the help of a few other detail parts). You *could* do this but it would be a lot of work. These parts are more useful for locomotive upgrading and detail changes.

On the right side of the EMD hood there are several details that are also offered by Cannon. Cannon calls them an EMD Door & Plate. On some models these details are cast a little thin. If you wish to improve these details, you must remove the old parts. Scrape off the old doors, sand the area smooth, and cement the new parts into place.

Air intake screens. Some long hood details include air intake screens. These are located just to the rear of the cab along the top of the hood on second-generation EMD units. On GE and Alco Century units these screens are located near the rear of the unit. Some GEs also have screens, located more toward the front of the long hood, that provided air for the equipment blower.

Upgrading the air intake screens on EMD units is quite easy, as Cannon & Co. has a line of replacement screens to fit many applications. Remove the old screen so it is flush with the hood

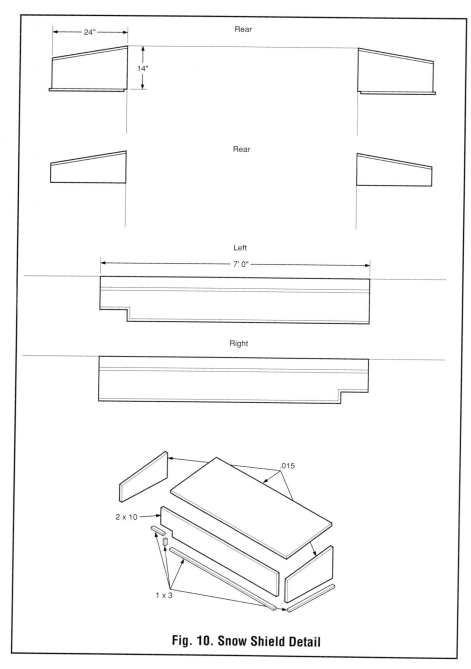

Rear

24"

14"

Rear

Left

7' 0"

Right

.015

2 x 10

1 x 3

Fig. 10. Snow Shield Detail

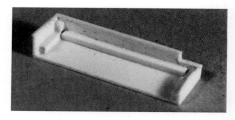

5-39. The inside of the scratchbuilt CN GP40-2W snow shields shows the Evergreen 4" x 4" bracing.

5-40. The left snow shield is installed on an Athearn GP40 with a Detail Associates Canadian cab.

surface by filing, scraping, and sanding the area smooth.

Changing intake screens on a GE unit is more difficult, as there are no replacement parts available. Some manufacturers have the modeler in mind when designing locomotives. The Rail Power C30-7 shell has a full complement of intake screens on the long hood. Most railroads that have the C30-7 did not order the units with all

the screens, so you can remove the unused screens to match the prototype locomotive. You must cut any other intake screen additions from an unused shell, file them to the proper thickness, and attach them to the locomotive.

Louvers. Older first-generation EMD and Alco units took in all engine air through louvers in the hood doors. Certain locomotives models have specific louver arrangements. By altering

the louver arrangement you can in some cases change a locomotive from one type to another.

The GP7 and early versions of the GP9 were very similar except for the location of the hood door louvers. It is possible to change a GP7 to a GP9 and vice versa by removing or adding louvers. Detail Associates has a sheet of replacement louvers that only need to be cut out and cemented in the proper location. Removing louvers is no harder than scraping away the unwanted parts and smoothing the area with sandpaper (photo 5-38).

This technique is useful in converting Walthers GP9M, which is a chopped-nose, to a GP7 version of this locomotive, of which there are no available models.

Snow shields. Several northern railroads, most notably Canadian National and CP Rail, have installed snow shields over the internal filter screens on some EMD units. Details West has a part they call an awning included with

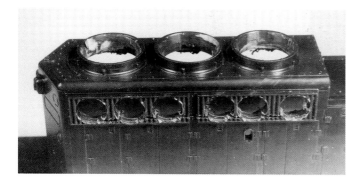

5-41. To detail this Athearn SD40-2 to match an early unit, you will have to replace the cast-on grill. To remove the grill, drill a number of ¼" holes in it. Cut out the sections between the holes with a razor saw. The bottom cut has already been made. You can also update the fans. Use a ½" bit to drill out the center section of the fans.

5-42. Remove the remaining portion of the grill with a mill file. Also remove the fan housings. Since the new parts have a mounting flange, carefully size the opening to accommodate the new part without leaving any gaps.

5-43. Install the new grill and the fans in the openings. If carefully done, the new parts will look as though they have been cast in place.

a smoke deflector set. This awning is used as a snow shield on some CP Rail GP38-2 units. The CN snow shields are a little more difficult because they are a different style than the CP parts. These shields have been fitted to a number of SD40-2s, GP38, and 40-2Ws. Figure 10 shows the dimensions of the parts required. The assembled shields are braced in the inside with pieces of Evergreen 4 x 4 to strengthen the joints (photo 5-39). Photo 5-40 shows the left shield installed on a GP40-2W. These shields are also offered as detail parts by Custom Finishing.

Radiator intake grills. Another hood-side detail is the radiator air intake grills (photos 5-41, 5-42, 5-43). On all units these grills are located at the rear of the long hood. For EMD units, Cannon & Co. offer a line of radiator grills. You can use these to improve, update, or backdate locomotives. Using the proper Cannon parts, you can update an Athearn GP38-2, which represents an early production model to a later

model. Remove the cast-on internal filter screens and radiator grills from the model. Install the proper Cannon grills following their instructions. With these changes, the model will represent a later production unit.

Blower ducts. All EMD units from the GP30 on have a unique part on the left side of the rear hood. This is the traction motor blower housing. This housing is modeled quite well on most locomotives, but our friends at Cannon & Co. have an extensive line of absolutely correct housings that can replace the cast-on parts. The primary housing is the "angled" or "free-flow" blower housing. Starting in 1983 EMD began putting this housing on all production units. All GP38-2s, 39s, 40-2s, 49s, 50s, and SD40-2s delivered from 1983 on carried this part. The Athearn models of the GP38-2, 40-2 , 50, and SD40-2 have the older housing. To model any of these as post-1983 units, you must remove and replace the old blower duct with the Cannon part. Use the Cannon instruc-

tions to remove the old housing and add the new. While it is not part of the housing detailing, changing this part will require altering the handrails as well.

Water sight glass. Starting in 1972 with the dash 2 series of GP38, 40, SD38, and 40 locomotives, EMD began installing water-level sight glasses on the right side of the long hood. This is the oval opening slightly below the radiator grills. On the prototype this opening is covered with glass. To simulate glass in this opening use Micro-Scale Kristal Kleer. Do this after you complete the locomotive. Paint the raised gasket around the opening black and then glaze the opening. Use a toothpick to apply the Kristal Kleer around the opening until the thick white material covers the opening. When the material dries it will be clear.

Miscellaneous hood details. There are many miscellaneous details that can be applied to the hood sides. Some are common details, while some are railroad specific.

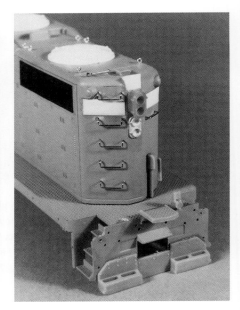

5-44. The rear of a heavily kitbashed ATSF SD26 shows the many detail parts that have been added. You will need to build up the Detail Associates end ladders with etched brass side rails and brass wire rungs. Solder the delicate pieces together carefully.

5-45. Replace the rear nose of this Rail Power SD45 shell with a more accurate and detailed Cannon part. Using the new part as a guide, remove the old nose so that the new part fits nicely into the opening with a minimum of filling, filing, and sanding.

5-46. Here is a rear view of Southern Pacific GP9E, which was backdated from a Proto 2000 GP18 locomotive. Replace the cast plastic grabs supplied with the locomotive with new wire grab irons and blank out the number boards with .010 sheet styrene.

Most EMD second-generation units have lift rings located at the back lower corner of the radiator grills. I overlooked this detail for years. Drill a no. 80 hole just below the rear corner of the radiator grill and install a Detail Associates wire eyebolt on each side. Use a prototype photo if in doubt about the location.

On EMD GP and SD50s and 60s there are a pair of short lifting tabs near the corners of each radiator grill. On Athearn GP50s and 60s these tabs are correctly modeled. The Rail Power SD60 shell does not have these tabs. Detail Associates has a set of the proper tabs. Mount them with liquid cement.

Some railroad-specific items include hood- or roof-mounted bells. Several railroads, such as Missouri Pacific and Milwaukee Road, mounted bells on the left side of the high hood. Photo 5-26 shows the bell placement behind the cab on a Milwaukee GP38-2. A number of railroads also mounted bells on their locomotive roofs. Locations and styles varied, so

always consult prototype information for accurate style and placement.

REAR NOSE

The rear nose (5-44) is usually just a taller version of what's up front. The usual details include grab irons, headlights, class lights, and number boards, although the rear class lights and number boards are slowly becoming a thing of the past.

Beside just adding the usual details to the rear nose and calling it good, Cannon & Co. offers a number of different rear-nose replacements for EMD units. To replace the rear nose on a unit, remove everything that the Cannon nose covers. It works best to saw out the old nose, staying slightly away from the finished cut line. When you finish sawing, go over it with a file. Test-fit the new part often. Cement the new nose in place and fill any gaps and sand it smooth. Using this method, I replaced the rear nose on a Rail Power SD45 shell (photo 5-45). I left the back of the flared radiator intact and

blended it into the top on the new nose with filler. With careful filling and finishing there is no trace of the joints.

Many railroads are now blanking out rear number boards. This is done in a variety of ways. Some are merely painted over. Some are plated over with sheet steel (photo 5-46), and some are filled in and repainted until no trace of them is visible.

ROOFS

The roofs (photo 5-47) on the long hoods offer a large variety of details and again, as on other areas, there are significant differences between EMD roof details and those found on virtually all other locomotives. As mentioned before, the basic mechanical principal is the same among all builders, but the layout and mechanical details differ.

Internal filter hatches. One trademark of second generation EMD units is the location of the air filter equipment. On virtually all units from the GP30 on there is some type of internal filter hatch located right behind the locomotive cab. While many hatches look similar, there are quite a number of variations on different models. These filter hatches are a cast-on detail on body shells and most are quite accurate. On some shells, most notably those from Rail Power, these hatches are a little "flat" and poorly detailed. These hatches can be replaced with accurate parts from Cannon. They offer virtually every type of standard EMD hatch from the GP30 up to the SD70. File the old hatch down to the base of the roof and install the new hatch. If you want the most accurate unit possible, there is no excuse when it comes to the filter hatch.

Paper filters. The GP and SD38 locomotives used a paper air filter instead of the conventional EMD internal filter. This filter appears on these units as a rectangular box structure behind the internal filter hatch. An option on these locomotives was an angled filter box, which several railroads ordered. Cannon makes such an angled filter box. To add this part you must remove the existing box. The more care you take in removing the old box and fitting the new, the less filling you will need to do for a good fit. If you don't want to go through this process, carefully file the corners of the box at a 45-degree angle until the bottom edge of the box is even with the top edge of the roof. If you trim carefully, you can alter the left side access door to look like the smaller door on the prototype angled filter box.

Paper air filters were also used on some rebuilt units. Illinois Central began adding paper air filters to its rebuilt GP7 and 9 units in 1969. A variety of filter housing styles were used. Several other railroads, most notably Conrail, Southern Pacific, and Milwaukee, added paper filters to some of their rebuilts also.

When modeling these details it is important to work from prototype photos, as there are many variations of the filter housings. In model form there are several styles available. Custom Finishing has a "Horst" filter. This unit looks like a yoke over the top of the hood. Detail Associates also offers this part as well as several others, including a low profile "dynacell" filter (photo 5-48), as applied to the sides of the rebuilt units. Other filter housings will have to be scratchbuilt.

Dynamic brakes. Dynamic brakes are applied to many locomotives as a braking feature. On GE units they are mounted internally and are difficult to spot. Alco usually mounted them over the engine with only grills on the side and a long vent on top of the hood denoting their presence. EMD dynamic brakes, on the other hand, are very visible. From the GP7 through the GP60 their presence is marked by flared bulges in the hood over the engine with grills on the sides and one or two cooling fans on the roof.

Modeling dynamic brakes is easy, as most units come standard with this part. On many recently released locomotives you have the choice of either dynamic or nondynamic units. The most common problem modeling dynamic brakes is removing them from units that are not equipped with them. Athearn models, starting with the SD40-2 introduced in the early 1980s, have a removable dynamic brake hatch. This is easily replaced with a nondynamic brake hatch that the model comes with or which can be ordered from Athearn. Photo 5-49 shows identical Milwaukee Road GP38-2s except one has dynamic brakes and one has none. These nondynamic hatches serve as raw material for those models where there is no nondynamic brake option. The Rail Power SD45 locomotive is an example of such a unit.

Only one railroad, the CNW, ordered the SD45 without dynamic brakes. To model one of these unique units, remove the cast-on brake blister. This process is compounded by the SD45 flared radiator housing, which extends into this area. Cut out the entire dynamic brake area with a razor saw from just behind the internal filter hatch back to just in front of the fan mounting plate. Remove the front tapered portion of the flared radiator from the hatch, which will be reinstalled later. File the opening down to

5-47. As seen in this rear hood view of ATSF SD26, mount all air tanks, plumbing, fans, grab irons, and bell.

5-48. A paper air filter box is a common detail on some rebuilt GP7 and 9 models. Install a Detail Associates "dynacell" filter on a Proto 2000 GP18 that will be backdated to a rebuilt GP9.

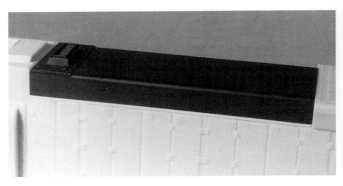

5-49. This roof detail on two Athearn GP38-2s, detailed for the Milwaukee Road, indicates the difference between units equipped with dynamic brakes and those equipped with nondynamic brakes.

5-50. Remove the cast-on dynamic brake from this Rail Power SD45 shell to make it a Chicago & Northwestern SD45. Make the new nondynamic brake hatch from two Athearn nondynamic brake hatches from the Athearn SD40-2 because a single hatch is not long enough. Cut the dynamic brake fairings from the removed area so they can be added to the front of the radiators later.

the top of the hood doors. This opening is longer than the SD40-2 nondynamic hatch, so you must splice a second hatch to make up the extra length. Fit the lengthened hatch into the opening (photo 5-50) and cut the previously removed tapered flared sections to the proper length and cement them into place. Fill and sand all gaps.

One of the few details that can be improved on some dynamic-brake-equipped units are the fans. A host of new see-through fans makes this a worthwhile endeavor. Removing the old fans can be quite tedious. The quickest and easiest method I know to remove 48" fans is to drill up through the bottom of the fan casting with a 1/2" bit. This leaves only the outside edge and mounting flange. Then shave off the remaining edge and mounting flange with a no. 17 blade (photo 5-51). Prepare the new fan by removing any flash and traces of the casting sprue, installing the fan blade, and cementing the properly oriented fan in place.

Dynamic brake vent. Another detail associated with the EMD dynamic brake is a brake vent. This detail first appeared in 1972 on the dash 2 models and is located between the dynamic brake fan and the front radiator fan. On the Athearn SD40-2 and SD40T-2 this vent is represented by a square chunk of plastic. On the subsequent Athearn units, the GP38-2, GP40-2

etc., this vent is properly modeled. The SD40-2 vent can be replaced with a Details West part or you can scratchbuild one from two pieces of sheet styrene.

Radiator fans. There are quite a few types of radiator fans with certain types often specific to certain locomotives. Many of the newer model locomotives have beautiful cast-on fans and there is nothing to be gained by replacing them. For older, less detailed locomotives, a number of manufacturers offer quite an array of fans for almost any application. There are several reasons for changing fans on locomotives. New fans may have better detail than existing cast-on fans, or the fans may not match those on a prototype locomotive.

You can remove the cast-on fans following the same procedure as used for the dynamic brake fans. Rail Power includes the fans on their shells as separate parts, making replacement a snap. When upgrading fans on an older prototype locomotive work from a photo of the prototype. Railroads often mix different styles of EMD fans indiscriminately when shopping a locomotive, as long as the fan is the same size and mounted similarly. Using more than one type of fan on a locomotive makes an interesting conversation piece, as long as the application is accurate.

Alco RS and RSD units also have a roof fan. These have a single large fan with the housing extending up from

the locomotive roof, covered with a large grill. There is not much that can be done on these units except to replace the cast-on grill with a Detail Associates grill.

All GE and Alco Century units have the radiators mounted near the roof, covered with a large grill. The cooling fan is inside the rear hood and is not visible. This leaves little to do in this area as far as improving detail.

Winterization hatches. A winterization hatch is sometimes added to the roof of EMD units. This hatch covers the front radiator fan and is installed on some northern locomotives to allow the crew or maintenance forces to close a shutter on the hatch to keep the cooling water warmer. CP Rail, CNW, and Soo all have some locomotives equipped with this option.

Details West has a good selection of hatches for many applications. You can apply these plastic hatches right over the fans in some cases. Several of these castings are metal, in which case you must remove the fan to be covered. After you remove the fan, fit the hatch carefully over the jog between the roof and the fan mounting plate (photo 5-52). Before these particular details were released by Details West I made several hatches for my CNW GP50s. I made them from strip and sheet styrene and used fine brass screen for the center section, hoping

5-51. Use a no. 17 X-acto blade to carefully cut the lip away from a fan mounting flange on this Bachmann Spectrum F40PH shell. You can use the same technique to remove the dynamic brake fans.

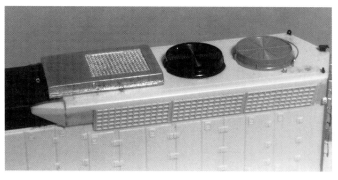

5-52. The radiator area of a Rail Power SD45 shell has new detail parts, such as fans, a winterization hatch, lift rings, and grab irons.

for a see-through effect. There is little or none, so I now use the cast parts.

Exhaust stacks. Exhaust stacks are a significant roof detail, especially on the newer dash 8 and 9 GE units, which resemble a bathtub in both shape and size. There are two types of exhaust stacks, turbocharged and nonturbocharged. EMD units without a turbocharger have more than one exhaust stack, except for a few models of SW switchers. The entire E and F unit series, the GP7, 9, some 15s, 18, 28, and 38, as well as the SD7, 9, 18, 28, and 38 series all lack turbochargers. These units all have two small exhaust stacks on the roof. On some rebuilt units railroads added two more stacks and called this feature a "liberated exhaust" (photo 5-53).

Modeling the nonturbo units exhaust stacks is easy because these parts either look good as is or can easily be replaced with Detail Associates EMD nonturbo stacks. A nice touch when modeling these stacks is to open up the middle down through the roof to represent the exhaust opening. This is more of a consideration on some GP and SD38 units. The exhaust stack lip on some of these units is only slightly above the base plate, and if you leave the base closed the exhaust stack will look as though it is plugged. To open the stack, drill several holes through the inside of the stack and finish the job with needle files. Some railroads in fire-prone regions added spark ar-

restors to the nonturbo stacks. Both Details West and Detail Associates make several styles of these parts designed to fit SW switchers and all models of E, F, GP, and SD units. Follow the manufacturers' instructions when adding these details.

Turbocharged stacks are even more interesting because there are a wide variety of styles from various manufacturers. GE offers a greater variety of stacks. Athearn does a good job representing these stacks on their extensive line of EMD units. Some Rail Power shells and even the expensive Kato SD40 lack the Athearn accuracy. While there are some detail parts out there, the best way to improve these

substandard details is to replace them with Athearn stacks. For a couple of bucks you can buy a hatch and remove the stack. This fact becomes even more significant when modeling GP and SD40-2 units built after 1980. After that time exhaust silencers were required. This type of stack is available on the Athearn GP50 hatch. A little work removing the stacks from the respective shells, and the new stack is easily installed.

GE exhaust stack modeling can get interesting, as there is less standardization than on EMD units. The most important step to modeling an accurate stack is to have good photos of the prototype locomotive.

5-53. The four nonturbo exhaust stacks on the roof of this rebuilt GP7 are called "liberated exhaust" by the rebuilders. Not all rebuilt locomotives have this feature, so check prototype photos carefully. Remove the cast-on stacks and replace them with Detail Associates parts so they all match.

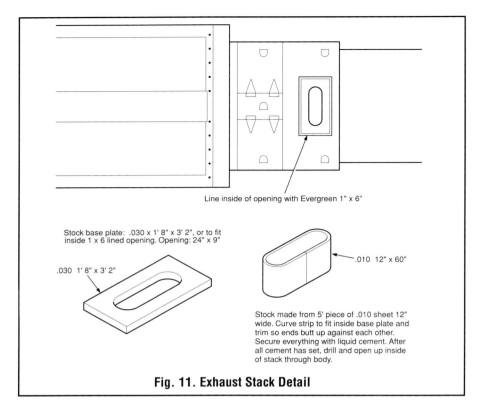

Line inside of opening with Evergreen 1" x 6"

Stock base plate: .030 x 1' 8" x 3' 2", or to fit
inside 1 x 6 lined opening. Opening: 24" x 9"

.030 1' 8" x 3' 2"

.010 12" x 60"

Stock made from 5' piece of .010 sheet 12"
wide. Curve strip to fit inside base plate and
trim so ends butt up against each other.
Secure everything with liquid cement. After
all cement has set, drill and open up inside
of stack through body.

Fig. 11. Exhaust Stack Detail

Most model GE locomotives come with a somewhat accurate version of their particular stack. Unfortunately for the GE modeler, there is not a good single source of replacement stacks. About the best stack on the market for many U and dash 7 locomotives is a cast-brass part from Utah Pacific. The modeler must find replacement parts from other shells. Rail Power GE shells feature separate stack castings that you can modify to fit many applications. Another way is to scratchbuild a stack. This is not as difficult as it may sound.

Figure 11 illustrates the building sequence for a BN C30-7 stack. Build it with Evergreen styrene sheet and strips for a credible-looking part.

Some models of Alco locomotives also have stack variations. Some early RS and RSD units had their stacks altered when Alco switched from air-cooled turbochargers to water-cooled units. The stack was moved from a lengthwise off-center orientation to a crosswise-centered mount. There were also detail differences on some stacks. Both Custom Finishing and Precision Scale offer several types of stacks for the RS and RSD units. Alco Century units have short, nearly flush stacks that are available through several manufacturers.

Air tanks. There are a few cases in which the locomotive air tanks are mounted on the roof of the unit. The was purposely planned only on EMD's SD24. Four air tanks were lined up side by side on the roof just behind the cab. Santa Fe owned a large number of these units and when they rebuilt them, they separated the tanks and located them along the sides of the roofs, two per side. Some interesting plumbing connected these tanks.

For a lack of space, several other roof mountings were used in the fuel tank area of certain models because of

5-54. Roof-mounted air tanks are not a common prototype detail. The lower unit is a CNW GP7. Use the .033 brass wire to plumb the Detail Associates Double 12" tanks. The top unit is an ATSF SD26. The Detail Associates 15" tanks are heavily modified. Plumb them with .022 brass wire.

5-55. Install lift tabs along the edge of the long hood of CN GP40-2W. While you could bend Detail Associates plastic tabs to represent these tabs, it is best if you make them from thin brass sheet for strength.

railroad-specified options. Some GP7, 9, and 35 models were so equipped. Again, refer to prototype photos for specific applications and locations. Photo 5-54 shows a photo of two roof air-tank applications.

Lift rings and tabs. A notable small detail on EMD and GE roofs are the lift tabs and lift rings or eyebolts. On some EMD locomotives the lift rings are represented by small blobs of plastic or are nonexistent. Fortunately, parts manufacturers make a variety of these items. To model the EMD rings remove the cast-on blobs if present and drill holes in these locations. On later Athearn units the blobs are absent but the lift ring locations are denoted by a small depression where you can drill. Detail Associates offers two types of lift rings, plastic and wire. The plastic parts are more prototypical but they are quite fragile. The wire eyebolts are very durable. You can install them in no. 80 holes and secure them with CA.

Some EMD units have roof tabs instead of eyebolts. Detail Associates has both short and long tabs included in the same package. To install these tabs on the roof you will need to inset them in the roof before cementing to give the mounting some strength. If you merely cement the end to the roof I can almost guarantee that the tabs will break off when handled. Figure 12 shows how to insert these parts for a stronger mounting. These tabs were not used on many locomotives, so work from prototype photos for accurate usage.

Another unique style of mounting tabs is on some CN units (photo 5-55). These are similar to the long Detail Associates tabs but are mounted along the sides of the long hood to fit the contour of the edge of the hood. You could form the styrene Detail Associates parts to this shape, but new tabs made from thin sheet brass would be better. Use fig. 13 as a guide for making and bending these parts.

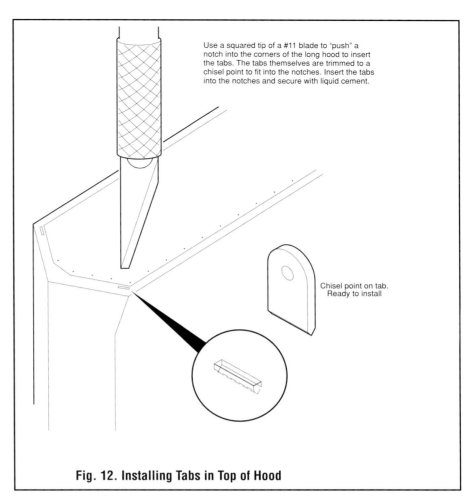

Fig. 12. Installing Tabs in Top of Hood

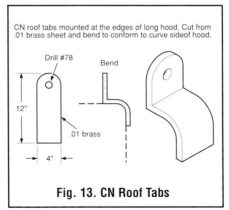

Fig. 13. CN Roof Tabs

On this CN GP40-2W the anti-glare panel, window gaskets, class lights, grab irons, and other small details have been accurately painted to reflect the appearance of the actual unit.

6 Painting and Finishing

You can build or buy the most exquisitely detailed locomotive ever made, but unless it is painted and finished properly it will look no better than those toy train locomotives at the discount store. A good paint job requires proper preparation and proper application. Whether you are doing touch-up work with a small brush or a full-blown multi-colored air brush job, you must be careful to do the job right.

There are several excellent books on the subject of painting, including *Painting and Weathering Railroad Models* by Jeff Wilson, which includes the basic instructions you need to brush-paint, airbrush, remove paint, and create realistic weathering on your locomotives and other railroad models. Although *Painting and Weathering Railroad Models* is a very thorough reference, there are still a number of locomotive painting and finishing issues to cover in this chapter.

DETAILING A FACTORY-PAINTED MODEL

As manufacturers have introduced ever more detailed and accurate locomotives, they have also improved the paint and finish of those locomotives. Not many years ago, a serious modeler wouldn't have been caught dead with a factory-painted locomotive on his layout. Times have changed. Some of today's newest releases are painted and marked so well it is difficult to tell the difference between a custom-painted unit and one that was factory-painted.

The main difference between factory paint and custom paint is how details are added to a unit. When a unit is custom-painted, all parts and details are the same shade of the particular colors scheme. When detailing a factory-painted unit problems can arise. It seems manufacturers use their own particular shade of a specific railroad color, and it is often difficult to match a particular shade with off-the-shelf railroad colors. If you can match factory colors or come reasonably close, you will have a better chance of success with such a project.

Matching paint, or at least coming quite close, is not very difficult. Choose a similar color of your favorite brand of paint and make a test swatch, just as they do at the hardware store. Never compare wet paint to dry paint. Let the paint dry and then compare. If the color is noticeably different, use an eyedropper and put some of the paint into a separate mixing cup so the entire bottle is not contaminated. Add several drops of a lighter or darker color as the case dictates and make another test swatch. Don't automatically use white and black as the lightener and darkener. It's often best to use other colors to get a particular shade. Always note the proportion of paint colors you mix and keep notes of the changes so you can repeat the color if you need to. Sometimes you will need to mix more than two colors.

It is not always necessary to match the colors exactly. Weathering will often blend slightly different colors together. When you are satisfied with the color match, the project can move forward.

You can apply the paint to the details with either an airbrush (if some of the parts are larger) or a brush. In fact, you can use a brush for the entire project as long as you use acrylic paints. The Athearn SD40-2 in Conrail paint is a brush-detailed job. This engine started as a stock Athearn factory-painted unit. The overall Athearn locomotive is a dead ringer for an actual Conrail unit, with the exception of the front anti-climber and truck sideframes. I added the larger parts, the anti-climber, and the signal box to the model and painted it Conrail Blue with Badger Modelflex acrylic paint. This is a very close match to the Athearn paint without custom mixing. Add other small details such as a new horn, grab irons, lift rings, and an antenna—also painted blue. Add buffer plates, coupler cut levers, M.U. hoses, and a front plow to the pilot. Paint these items, the pilots and steps, air tanks, and number boards Model Flex Engine Black. Use a small

6-1. This Conrail SD40-2 is a factory-painted Athearn unit with a number of applied details. The details, including the entire underframe, have been brush-painted with Badger's Modelflex. Brush marks are hardly visible on the larger details. Using this method of detailing, you can build good-looking locomotives without starting from scratch.

brush to pick out the small details. Paint the headlights, class lights, and side window frames silver; the window, number board gaskets, and the inside of the exhaust stack black; and the step ends of the handrails and edge of the bottom step white.

Smooth the fuel tank on the SD40-2 chassis with a file, apply fuel fittings, and brush-paint them black. Instead of running the brush strokes the length of the tank, I ran them vertically down the sides of the tank. Any remaining brush marks will appear to be the streaks that prototypically wash down the sides of the tank. Modify the truck frames to look like the older Flex-i-coil sideframes. Add brake lines and speed recorder and paint them black.

Add small data decals, seal them with Dullcote spray, do some weathering and cab glazing, and the project is complete. After reassembly you have a finished model (photo 6-1) that was completed with nothing more than detail parts, a few tools, and paint brushes, and compares favorably with custom-painted units.

PRIMER

When you are preparing to paint or repaint your detailed model, it is critical that you use a primer coat. This coat will greatly improve your chances of a successful paint job, especially with a light-colored paint. Some of the new acrylics are touted as needing no primer, but don't believe it. While it is true that enough coats of anything will eventually result in a solid, even color, the resulting thick coat of paint will begin to obscure details. Black, grays, dark browns, and dark blues can cover adequately by themselves, but try spraying a light, translucent color like CNW Zito Yellow over a black plastic shell with white styrene modifications. It will take at least a dozen coats to achieve the same paint hue over both the black and white surfaces. After you use a primer, which contains an opaque pigment, the light yellow will cover well in just a few coats with a thin finish (photo 6-2). Even if you use a dark color, you should use a primer coat. When detailing or modifying a model you usually have to do some filling, filing, or sanding to smooth surfaces or blend in new details. Oftentimes what appeared to be a perfect, blemish-free surface, turns out to be anything but that when paint is applied. A primer coat helps you to find these areas and fix them before you apply the finish coat. Sand off the primer in the affected area, repair, and reprime the area.

6-2. It is best to prime all models before applying the final color. This not only provides a good base for any color, it makes any surface defects visible so you can repair them before you apply a final coat of paint.

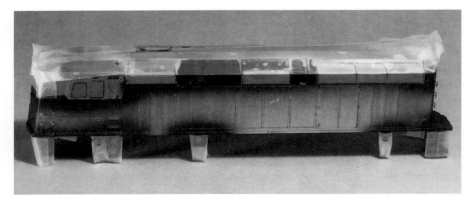

6-3. Mask this F40PH shell before applying the second color. Typically, it is best to apply darker colors over lighter ones. However, in this case I suggest you paint a light color (silver) over a dark color (black). There are two reasons for this. One, silver is an opaque color that will easily cover any undercoat. Two, the color separation lines on the AMTRAK color scheme make it difficult to mask the unit if silver is applied first.

MASKING

Unless you model only single-color locomotives, you will need to be able to separate colors when painting. Expert brush painters may be able to paint a nice straight line without help, but the rest of us need some help. If you use an airbrush, you will need to mask the separation line with tape. Most modelers use masking tape, but I find it difficult to work with, because it must be trimmed to get a good "hard" edge, and I sometimes find that the sol-vents in certain paints soften the masking tape adhesive, causing problems when I remove the tape. The adhesive can also be quite aggressive, sometimes lifting previously applied paint off a model. I prefer to use Scotch Brand Transparent Tape, because it provides a nice "hard" edge, can be cut easily, and conforms fairly well over details. Its adhesive is not as aggressive as that of some masking tapes. The Scotch Tape has another major advantage over even other transparent tapes. Its dull surface

helps you determine if the tape is in contact with the model surface. Tape in contact shows the underlying surface quite well, whereas noncontact areas show up as dull or creamy white. It is difficult to see if glossy or shiny transparent tapes are in contact, and opaque tapes don't help at all.

Masking is a straightforward process but can be difficult over irregular or detailed surfaces. This is one reason why you should leave grab irons off hood ends until after painting. They are difficult to mask over and around. Some paint schemes are also difficult to mask when there are more than two colors or when there are curved color separations. The main ingredient required here is patience. A simple scheme may be masked in a matter of minutes, but some difficult schemes will take hours and many small pieces to properly mask.

When applying tape for masking, it is usually best to start with the largest pieces. Carefully position each piece in the correct location before pressing it into place. The most important step in masking is to properly burnish the tape edges at the color separation lines. Only when the tape edge is in full contact will the paint not creep under the tape and ruin the paint job. You can use a number of items to burnish the tape. A pointed wooden stick works well for prodding the tape into corners and over details. The entire piece of tape need not be in complete contact with the surface, just the edges along the paint separation line.

When large areas must be masked it is not necessary to cover the entire area with the Scotch Tape. There are other less costly ways to cover some of these areas. I prefer aluminum foil for these areas. The foil is flexible and conforms to nearly any shape easily. Moreover, it is impenetrable by paint unless it is damaged. After you finish all the color separation lines, cut pieces of foil and lay them over the area to be covered with the edge of the foil about ¼" from the masked edge. Use another piece of Scotch Tape to secure the foil to the already-applied tape.

While all facets of model building are important, the most accurate model

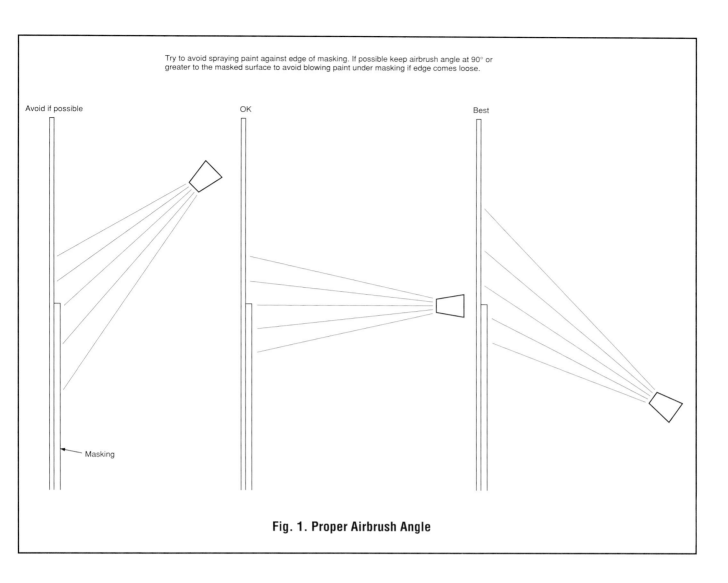

Try to avoid spraying paint against edge of masking. If possible keep airbrush angle at 90° or greater to the masked surface to avoid blowing paint under masking if edge comes loose.

Avoid if possible

OK

Best

Masking

Fig. 1. Proper Airbrush Angle

and smoothest, thinnest paint application is worthless unless the color separations are properly located and straight. Study prototype photos to determine color separations and plan the masking.

An important tip when airbrushing over masking is to avoid spraying down onto the masked edge. Try to keep the spray pattern either perpendicular to or below the edge if possible. This will reduce the chances of blowing paint under the masking should there be loose tape or details that the tape cannot conform to exactly. Figure 1 illustrates this. While this is not always possible, practicing this where possible will prevent future mistakes. Another tip is to use light coats of paint that dry rapidly. Heavy, slow-drying coats along

the masked edges can creep under the tape along hood doors and other engraved panel lines.

In a multiple masked scheme, such as that in photo 6-4, which requires at least two separate masking sessions, you might want to leave the first masking in place and simply mask for the third when the second color is dry. I prefer to remove the masking after each color. This serves two purposes. If the paint is allowed to dry hard, the masked edge may chip when the tape is removed. Also, any problems with the first masking such as bleed-under are easier to fix before another color is added.

When the paint has set up, usually several minutes for fast-drying paints and up to a half-hour for some slow-

drying paints, remove the masking. Be careful not to touch any of the freshly painted surfaces except on the masking, as the paint will still be soft. Gently pry up a corner of tape with the tip of a no. 11 X-acto blade and pull it back using tweezers. It is best not to pull the tape up but rather try to pull it back over itself at a sharp angle (fig. 2). It will be less likely to pull up any paint. Should there be any major problems with the masked edges, fix them before spraying the third color. Minor chips and bleed-unders can wait until all painting is done. You can touch them up then.

TOUCH-UP

When the paint has set properly, remove all masking carefully. It is likely

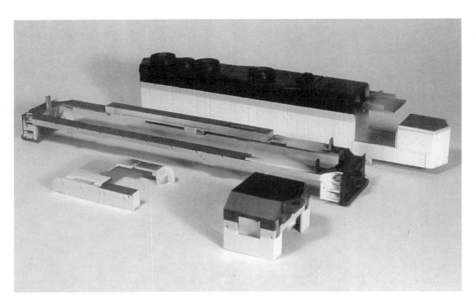

6-4. A multi-colored scheme, such as this Kato GP35 painted in Chessie System colors, will require a number of separate masking and painting sessions. Pay special attention to aligning the masking accurately so that the color separations all line up properly.

that there will be at least a few places where the paint crept under the masking. If the areas are small you can touch them up with the appropriate color of paint. Sometimes you can remove the paint gently with a cotton swab that has been dipped into a little paint thinner. Be careful not to damage any surrounding paint. Sometimes the offending paint can be gently scrapped with the tip of a no. 11 X-acto blade, especially in narrow grooves and crevices. If there is a large amount of blow-under or bleeding, you may need to re-mask the area and spray it again.

At this point you can brush-paint any number of small details. If you left off any grab irons you can install them now and paint them the appropriate color, as long as they won't interfere with decal application.

GLOSS COAT

When all paint has completely dried, you can apply the decals. Before doing this you will need to determine if the surface is properly prepared for decal application. The surface must have a gloss or semi-gloss finish. Many paints do leave such a surface when properly applied. Any paints that have a dull or flat finish must be given a gloss coat. Otherwise, decals applied over them will have a "silvery" look on their clear film areas that is impossible to fix.

If you need to add a gloss coating, it is easy to do with an airbrush. Several paint manufacturers offer a clear gloss coating. Be sure to follow any manufacturer's recommendation for thinning and application.

I use Testor's Glosscote for all my projects. I have never had a problem with paint compatibility, even over an acrylic base. The paint must be completely dry so the Glosscote and thinner will not react with the paint. Be sure the model surface is clean before you apply Glosscote. If it isn't clean, wash and dry it. All exposed model surfaces should be gloss-coated, even areas that will not have decals. The gloss coating also serves to "harden" the previously applied paint and provides an even, consistent surface for

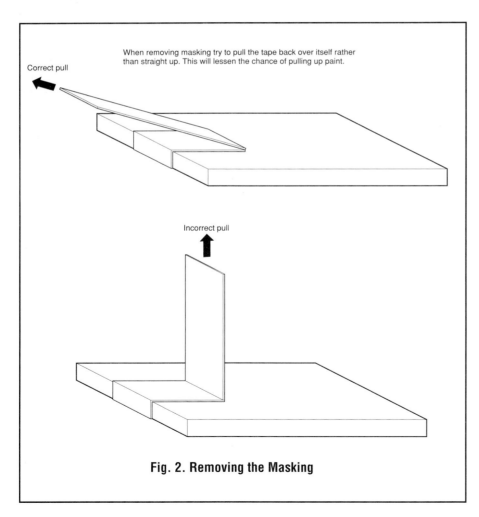

When removing masking try to pull the tape back over itself rather than straight up. This will lessen the chance of pulling up paint.

Correct pull

Incorrect pull

Fig. 2. Removing the Masking

6-5. The top decal is from a Microscale sheet. Each decal is printed on a separate piece of decal film. This film has a gradual taper to the edge so it will blend in more easily when applied to a model. The lower decals are from Herald King and are printed on a solid piece of decal film. Trim them as close to the decal as possible to minimize the film on the model surface.

6-6. Add small information and warning decals in appropriate places on a locomotive to make it look realistic. While assembling small numbers and letters to make an accurate decal may not be fun, the result may give a model that little extra that makes a good model exceptional.

weathering later. To use Glosscote, I mix a 50:50 ration of lacquer thinner and paint and spray it through an airbrush at about 25 psi. It will take several light coats to gloss a dull or flat surface. Cover the model with overlapping strokes, just as when applying color coats. You may need to adjust the lighting in the room so you can see the surface. The first coat of gloss will dry to a semi-gloss. After several minutes apply another coat. Repeat this several times until the surface stays a good semi-gloss or gloss. Set the parts aside to dry for a day before adding decals. The lacquer thinner and solvents must evaporate completely.

DECALS

The proper application of decals will turn your painted but unmarked model locomotive into a miniature of the real thing. Before applying decals, make sure the model surface is free of oil, dirt, and dust. Wash the parts if they need it. There is no need for the parts to be completely dry, as you can dry any water that interferes with decal placement with a soft cloth.

Before beginning, consult prototype photos to determine the exact location of the major decals. Accurate decal placement is essential to a first-class model. Some decal sheets are generic and are not accurate for all models, so check the decal sheets against prototype photos to determine discrepancies. If you notice size differences, check another manufacturer's sheet for the correct size decals. Plan decal placement so you don't have any surprises after the decal has been soaked and is awaiting placement.

I use the Microscale Model Finishing System for applying manufacturers' decals. Micro Set and Micro Sol do a great job. When beginning the decaling process, position the model so you can apply the decals to a surface that is as horizontal or flat as possible. This will lessen the chance of decals floating or sliding out of position. It is best to apply the largest decal first, especially when there are smaller decals to be applied in its immediate vicinity. This will prevent any overlap problem should the smaller decals be placed incorrectly. When cutting Microscale decals from the sheet, leave the extended edges of the clear decal film intact. They are tapered and when applied will blend well into the surrounding surface. Cutting the clear film will leave a sharper edge, which will be more difficult to hide. When using Herald King decals or any others that are printed on a solid sheet of clear film, trim as close as possible to each decal (photo 6-5).

In some instances the applied decal may appear to be thin or translucent, especially if it is a light-colored decal applied over a dark surface. This was the case when I built a Santa Fe SD26. When I applied the large yellow Santa Fe letters to the blue sides of the long hoods, the color of the letters appeared weak or thin compared to the rich yellow of the rest of the unit. After spending many hours kitbashing this unit, I couldn't settle for such a glaring difference in colors. After contemplating hand-painting over the letters with the proper color paint, I decided to try another set of decals over the first, since the Microscale sheet I used had several sets. Instead of trying to apply the entire large decal over the existing letters, I cut the separate letters from the sheet. When I applied the first letter and placed it on top, I saw a rich color that perfectly matched the yellow paint. I applied the rest of the letters and the problem was solved.

When the decals have dried completely use a damp cloth or tissue to wipe off any decal adhesive that may remain on the model. This adhesive appears as a dull film around some

6-7. Use thin washes of paint to give depth to louvers and grills. The paint pigment will settle into the low areas quite nicely.

decals and should be removed to properly finish the model. Again, check for any decal flaws that can be corrected with Micro Sol. Sometimes small holes or cracks in the decal film can develop around details. Use a matching color paint and touch up these areas.

When everything has dried for a day, seal the model surface. Sealing it will blend the decal film into the surrounding paint and provide a base for weathering the model. First, you must determine the type of finish. Models that represent newer units can be sealed with a gloss coating, while those representing older units can be sealed with a flat finish.

Again, I prefer Testor's Glosscote for glossy areas and its counterpart, Dullcote, for flat areas. Both products are thinned and applied in the same way. Be sure to thoroughly shake the Dullcote bottle so all the "dulling" material is suspended. Thin either product 50:50 with lacquer thinner and spray at 20 to 25 psi with an airbrush. These products are available in aerosol cans—but use them only if you do not have an airbrush, because they spray a heavy coat. Apply several light coats, letting the material dry several minutes before applying the next coat. Do this until both the decal and surrounding surface have the same appearance. The parts should be set aside in a dust-free

area to dry for a day before further work (photo 6-6).

WEATHERING

The world of the prototype locomotive is hostile. Dirt, smoke, rain, snow, sun, wind, use, and abuse all contribute to the appearance of a locomotive. That factory-fresh appearance does not last much longer than the first trip down the rails. While some railroads do wash and maintain the exterior of their fleets, the forces of man and nature quickly leave their mark on even the best-maintained units. Unless you want to build mint-condition locomotives for display, you will need to add some light weathering.

Many factors contribute to the appearance of a locomotive. Dirt and soot leave their own particular marks, as does weathering like fading paint and rust. Additionally, use and abuse leave worn, chipped, dented, scratched, heat-faded, and blistered surfaces.

Railroad maintenance plays a major role in the locomotive's appearance. These factors include how often a locomotive is washed, whether or not it is repainted, or how well its colors weathers. A most notable example was Chicago & North Western's "Zito," or bright yellow, of the 1980s. When freshly applied it was a bright eye-catching yellow. After several years of

exposure it became a pale, chalky shadow of its former self.

Prototypically duplicating weathering requires more that just attacking a model indiscriminately with a random variety of weathering colors. Maybe you've seen model locomotives that look as though they've gone through the swamp rather than down the tracks, and the modeler thinks it looks great. While there are many heavily weathered locomotives in the real world, the vast majority are in far better shape. Most weathering effects are subtle and the key to successful weathering is your ability to reproduce those effects. A good prototype photo or personal observations of a train are necessary to do a good job. Only by studying the prototype can you hope to duplicate that "used" look.

Fading paint. Many times how a locomotive will be weathered is of little concern when you paint and decal the unit. You can duplicate many weathering effects over a normally painted or factory-painted unit. In some cases you must consider and adjust the locomotive's basic colors to properly reproduce some weathering effects. Heavy color fading is an example. To properly reproduce the faded Chicago & North Western Zito Yellow you must mix and apply a faded yellow color. Apply the normal Chicago & North Western green, because this color does not fade nearly as much as the yellow. To heavily fade the Zito with a light weathering color would unprototypically fade the green areas, resulting in a unit that just does not look right.

Peeling paint. Another difficult effect to achieve is peeling paint. Small areas may be convincingly represented with small dabs of an appropriate underlying color, but larger areas simply do not look right with this method. To achieve good-looking peeled paint you must literally peel the paint from the surface as on the prototype. To do this the locomotive must first be painted with the base color showing beneath the peeled paint. Now the trick to peeling—apply petroleum jelly thickly with a brush to the areas that are to be peeled. Some modelers use rubber cement for this. Then apply the paint as you normally would. If you're using petroleum jelly, be careful when handling the unit so you don't disturb it. After the paint has set hard it can be peeled or wiped from the affected areas.

Weathering decals. You can also slightly weather decals. Do this before you seal or overcoat them. Use a very fine piece of sandpaper and gently rub the decal surface to remove some of the ink. This is a delicate process, so check the decal film often to make sure it is not damaged.

WEATHERING METHODS

There are two basic weathering mediums, paint and powdered chalk. Paint can be airbrushed, drybrushed, or applied as a wash, and powdered chalk can be applied with a brush. Where and how each material is used depends on the effects needed and your preference. Airbrushing is excellent for overall applications of a specific weathering color. It also works well for colors that blend or gradually fade away. Drybrushing works well for weathering that has a "harder" edge or defined area of coverage. Brushing powdered chalks is a combination of both air- and drybrushing and is useful for subtle effects and highlighting areas or parts.

The colors you use for weathering depends on what they are to represent. Some are quite easy. Black is used to represent soot and exhaust stains. Dark oranges and dark browns are used to reproduce different shades of rust. Other specific effects may not be quite as easy. Road grime color depends more on location than anything else. The color of the native soil is a significant contributor to the color of this weathering. The color of ballast dust contributes heavily to the appearance of the lower surfaces and trucks. Dust is blown up from the traction motor blowers and spray from wheels on wet track ends up on these surfaces.

Fading or weathering paint can get quite involved, as different colors and even different formulations of the same color weather differently. Some colors

6-8. Add subtle weathering on and around the truck area to make it look realistic. Several weathering colors have been applied to this MP GP15-1 truck to match a prototype photo. The results are worth the effort.

darken or deepen with age, while others fade. The weathering process is a multiple-step operation. It is not possible to do a realistic weathering job by mixing all the colors together and applying them to the model in one shot. Just as on the prototype, model weathering is done in layers. The basic paint color is weathered and then the dirt, grime, dust, spills, leaks, and wear areas are added over it.

Sealing or overcoating. Whether you have a factory-painted unit or one you painted and decaled, you must seal it with semi-gloss or flat to provide the proper base for weathering. This sealing was covered in the final step of the decaling process early in this chapter— you use it to blend the decals into the paint. It is best to use a flat or at least a semi-gloss sealer on your models. Most locomotives lose their glossy surface soon after delivery, and most weathering methods work better on a flat surface. Chalks will not stick to a gloss surface at all. Factory-painted units have pad printing of graphics (instead of decals), which leaves slightly raised areas of paint or ink. Apply a sealer to cover these raised areas and to leave a smooth surface on which to apply weathering.

Washes. A wash is nothing more than a very thin paint mixture you apply with a brush. The small amount of paint pigment in this highly thinned mix will naturally seek the lowest area to settle into. This is an effective method of highlighting or giving more depth to specific areas. Apply washes before weathering with an airbrush because a wash will quickly dissolve the weathering. A wash is very effective in giving locomotive grills, fans, and louvers more depth (photo 6-7). A good wash for these areas is a mixture of 10 percent black and 90 percent thinner. I prefer Floquil Engine Black thinned with mineral spirits rather than lacquer thinner. The area to receive the wash should be as level as possible. Otherwise, the wash may not spread evenly and the effect will be ruined. To apply a wash to the intake and radiator grills on an EMD locomotive, lay the shell on its side and apply it with a medium-sized soft brush. Start at one side of the grill and using a steady stroke go across the grill. The brush does not have to cover the entire grill, as capillary action will pull the thin paint over the entire grill. You may need to touch it up to achieve a balanced look. It may be best to practice this on an old shell to get the hang of it. Do not worry if some black paint remains on the top surfaces of the grills. When everything dries, use a soft cloth dampened with a little thinner to wipe these areas clean. Let the paint dry completely before turning the unit over and doing the other side.

Fans are similar to grills. The important thing is to try to get an even

6-9. Be sure to paint the faces of the wheels and the side of the truck without the sideframe in place. Notice the difference between the painted truck on the left and the unpainted truck on the right.

amount of wash on all fans so they appear similar. As on the grills, do not worry about paint remaining on the fan guards because you can remove it after the paint has dried.

Louvers are a little different from either grills or fans. For one thing, they are usually smaller. The other major difference is that you are trying to represent more of a shadow than depth. Use a smaller brush and a light hand when doing louvers. Just a touch to the louver will usually deposit enough mix with capillary action doing the rest. Louvers should also be perfectly level so the paint is distributed evenly.

Airbrushing. Using an airbrush is the most effective way to apply an even layer of color over a large surface. From the lightest, most subtle coats to heavy, thick deposits, the airbrush is the tool. The airbrush is good at applying subtle colors to smaller areas. It is also effective at creating exhaust deposits around the stack area, heavier road grime on truck, fuel tank, and pilot surfaces, and subtle streaks down the sides of units. With practice, you can apply even small details like grease stains around truck journals with an airbrush. The secret is to use very thin mixes of paint. Use the same mix of 10 percent paint to 90 percent thinner as you used with washes with the airbrush. Apply the paint in very thin coats and build up the effects

slowly. Even when modeling heavily weathered units, stick to thin coats. It is very difficult to remove too much weathering but always easier to add a little more (photos 6-8 and 6-9).

Drybrushing. Drybrushing is a process in which you pick up paint on a brush and wipe most of it off, leaving only traces, before applying it. This method is most useful for highlighting areas of complicated detail. Locomotive trucks are an area where this method can be most useful. These areas, while covered with details, are generally dark to start with and in shadows, making details difficult to see. Drybrushing with a lighter weathering color will pick out these details to give the trucks more depth.

Powdered chalks. Chalks are an effective means of duplicating some weathering effects. They come in a variety of colors in stick form and it's easy to powder them for application. Rub the sticks against coarse sandpaper or scrape the stick with a no. 11 X-acto blade. I usually scrape only enough for a single project, although you could make quite a pile and store it in small containers for future use.

Powdered chalks come in a variety of basic colors and you can mix them to reproduce almost any color. While it may seem unnecessary to have any colors but earth tones for weathering, you can mix some of the primary colors

with white or black to fade or darken appropriate locomotive colors without using an airbrush.

It's best to apply powdered chalks with a brush. The size and stiffness of the brush you use depend on the effects you want to achieve. You can achieve subtle effects by using a large soft brush. An old shaving-cream brush makes a great applicator. To apply heavier, more visible effects, use a stiffer brush. A small stiff brush works well to apply streaks down the sides of a unit.

You must seal or fix all chalks in place after they are applied, or they will be worn off by handling. Apply Testor's Dullcote mixed 50:50 with lacquer thinner with an airbrush, which works well as a sealer. As a rule of thumb, when chalk is sealed, dark-colored chalks remain about the same intensity while light-colored chalks fade dramatically. Light colors must be applied quite a bit more heavily to achieve the desired effect. If the light colors are not intense enough after sealing, apply more chalk and seal again.

FINAL SEALING

When all weathering is complete seal the surface again with your favorite clear overcoat. Again, a flat finish is usually the most realistic, although a semi-gloss finish would not be objectionable on a newer unit.

Chicago & North Western SD40
Manufactured by Kato

7 Diesel Shop
A Showcase of Locomotive Details

Kitbashed
Santa Fe SD26

Athearn frame and power train

Life-Like Proto 2000 cab, low nose, and sub-bases

Rail Power walkway–side sills, radiator

Con-cor rear two-thirds of long hood

Scratchbuilt air filter area of long hood

Chessie System GP35
Manufactured by Kato

Conrail SD40-2
Manufactured by Athearn

Amtrak F40PH
Manufactured by Life-Like

Burlington Northern C30-7
Manufactured by Rail Power (body) and Athearn (chassis)

Southern Pacific GP9E
Manufactured by Life-Like Proto 2000

Missouri Pacific GP15-1

Manufactured by Smokey Valley

Chicago & North Western SD45
Manufactured by Rail Power (body) and Overland (chassis)

Canadian National GP40-2W

Manufactured by Athearn

■Suppliers and Manufacturers

Some firms offer free catalogs or literature, others charge for their catalogs. Some railroad suppliers will sell direct to consumers and others sell only through hobby shops. Always check with your local hobby shop before trying to order direct from a manufacturer or importer. If you don't have a hobby shop in your area, there are a number of companies that sell parts and equipment by mail order. When corresponding with these manufacturers, be sure to include a self-addressed, stamped envelope.

A-Line (Proto Power West)
P. O. Box 7916
La Verne, CA 91750

Accu-paint (SMP Industries)
63 Hudson Rd., P. O. Box 72
Bolton, MA 01740

Athearn Inc.
19010 Laurel Park Rd.
Compton, CA 90222

Builders In Scale
P. O. Box 441432
Aurora, CO 80044

Cal-Scale
P. O. Box 322
Montoursville, PA 17754-0322

Cannon & Co.
310 Willow Heights
Aptos, CA 95003-9798

Champion Decal Co.
P. O. Box 1178
Minot, ND 58702

Con-Cor International
8101 E. Research Ct.
Tucson, AZ 85710

Detail Associates
P. O. Box 5357
San Luis Obispo, CA 93403

Details West
P. O. Box 61
Corona, CA 91718

Evergreen Scale Models
12808 N. E. 125th Way
Kirkland, WA 98034

Floquil-Polly S Color Corp.
Rt. 30 N.
Amsterdam, NY 12010

Grandt Line Products
1040-B Shary Ct.
Concord, CA 94518

Herald King Decals
P. O. Box 1133
Bettendorf, IA 52722

K&S Engineering
6917 W. 59th St.
Chicago, IL 60638

Kadee Quality Products
673 Avenue C
White City, OR 97503

Kato U.S.A., Inc.
100 Remington Rd.
Schaumburg, IL 60173

Keystone Locomotive Works
P. O. Box J
Pulteney, NY 14874

La Belle Industries
P. O. Box 328
Bensenville, IL 60106

Microscale Industries Inc.
P. O. Box 11950
Costa Mesa, CA 92627

Model Power
180 Smith St.
Farmingdale, NY 11735

Modelflex (Badger Airbrush Co.)
9128 W. Belmont
Franklin Park, IL 60131

NorthWest Short Line
P. O. Box 423
Seattle, WA 98111-0423

Overland Models Inc.
5918 Kilgore Ave.
Muncie, IN 47304

Pactra Hobby
1000 Lake Rd.
Medina, OH 44256

Plastruct
1020 S. Wallace Pl.
City of Industry, CA 91748

Precision Scale Co.
3961 Highway 93 N.
Stevensville, MT 59870

Run 8 Productions
P. O. Box 25224
Rochester, NY 14625

Smokey Valley Railroad Products
P. O. Box 339
Plantersville, MS 38862

Stewart Hobbies Inc.
P. O. Box 341
Chalfont, PA 18914

Testor Corp.
620 Buckbee St.
Rockford, IL 61104

Tichy Train Group
55 Kennedy Dr.
Hauppauge, NY 11788

Virnex Industries Inc.
S-2083 Herwig Rd.
Reedsburg, WI 53959

William K. Walthers, Inc.
P. O. Box 3039
Milwaukee, WI 53201-3039

■ Index